JUNIUS.

STAT NOMINIS UMBRA.

VOL. II.

LONDON:

Printed for HENRY SAMPSON WOODFALL,

in Pater Nofter Row.

MDCCLXXII.

Research Reprints Inc. · New York

First Published 1772
Reprinted 1970

LIBRARY OF CONGRESS CATALOG CARD NUMBER:
74-124793

PRINTED IN THE UNITED STATES OF AMERICA

LETTERS OF JUNIUS.

LETTER XXX.

TO THE PRINTER OF THE PUBLIC ADVERTISER.

SIR, 17. *October*, 1769.

IT is not wonderful that the great cauſe, in which this country is engaged, ſhould have rouſed and engroſſed the whole attention of the people. I rather admire the generous ſpirit, with which they feel and aſſert their intereſt in this important queſtion, than blame them for their indifference about any other. When the conſtitution is openly invaded, when the firſt original right of the people, from which all laws derive their authority, is directly attacked, inferior grievances naturally loſe their force, and are ſuffered to paſs by without puniſhment or obſervation. The preſent miniſtry are as ſingularly marked by their fortune, as by their crimes. Inſtead of atoning for their former conduct by any wiſe or popular meaſure, they have found, in the enormity of one fact, a cover and defence for a ſeries of meaſures, which muſt have been fatal to any other adminiſtration. I fear we are too remiſs in obſerving the whole of their proceedings. Struck with the principal figure, we do not ſufficiently mark in what manner the canvaſs is filled up. Yet ſurely it is not a leſs crime, nor leſs fatal in its conſequences, to encourage a flagrant breach of the law by a military force, than to make uſe of the forms of parliament to deſtroy the conſtitution.—The miniſtry ſeem determined to give us a choice of difficulties, and, if poſſible, to perplex us with the multitude of their offences. The expedient is worthy of the Duke of Grafton. But though he has preſerved a gradation and variety in his meaſures, we ſhould remember that the principle is uniform. Dictated by the ſame ſpirit, they deſerve the ſame attention. The following fact, though of the moſt alarming nature

ture, has not yet been clearly ſtated to the public, nor have the conſequences of it been ſufficiently underſtood. Had I taken it up at an earlier period, I ſhould have been accuſed of an uncandid, malignant precipitation, as if I watched for an unfair advantage againſt the miniſtry, and would not allow them a reaſonable time to do their duty. They now ſtand without excuſe. Inſtead of employing the leiſure they have had, in a ſtrict examination of the offence, and puniſhing the offenders, they ſeem to have conſidered *that* indulgence as a ſecurity to them, that, with a little time and management, the whole affair might be buried in ſilence, and utterly forgotten.

* A MAJOR general of the army is arreſted by the ſheriffs officers for a conſiderable debt. He perſuades them to conduct him to the Tilt-yard in St. James's Park, under ſome pretence of buſineſs, which it imported him to ſettle before he was confined. He applies to a ſerjeant, not immediately on duty, to aſſiſt with ſome of his companions in favouring his eſcape. He attempts it. A buſtle

* Major General Ganſel.

ensues. The bailiffs claim their prisoner. † An officer of the guards, not then on duty, takes part in the affair, applies to the ‡ lieutenant commanding the Tilt-yard guard, and urges him to turn out his guard to relieve a general officer. The lieutenant declines interfering in person, but stands at a distance, and suffers the business to be done. The officer takes upon himself to order out the guard. In a moment they are in arms, quit their guard, march, rescue the general, and drive away the sheriffs officers, who, in vain represent their right to the prisoner, and the nature of the arrest. The soldiers first conduct the general into the guard-room, then escort him to a place of safety, with bayonets fixed, and in all the forms of military triumph. I will not enlarge upon the various circumstances which attended this atrocious proceeding. The personal injury received by the officers of the law in the execution of their duty, may perhaps be atoned for by some private compensation. I consider nothing but the wound, which has been given to the law itself, to which no remedy has been applied, no satisfaction made.

† Lieutenant Dodd. ‡ Lieutenant Garth.

Neither

Neither is it my deſign to dwell upon the miſconduct of the parties concerned, any farther than is neceſſary to ſhew the behaviour of the miniſtry in its true light. I would make every compaſſionate allowance for the infatuation of the priſoner, the falſe and criminal diſcretion of one officer, and the madneſs of another. I would leave the ignorant ſoldiers entirely out of the queſtion. They are certainly the leaſt guilty, though they are the only perſons who have yet ſuffered, even in the appearance of puniſhment.* The fact itſelf, however atrocious, is not the principal point to be conſidered. It might have happened under a more regular government, and with guards better diſciplined than ours. The main queſtion is, in what manner have the miniſtry acted on this extraordinary occaſion. A general officer calls upon the king's own guard, then actually on duty, to reſcue him from the laws of his country; yet at this moment he is in a ſituation no worſe, than if he had not committed an offence, equally enormous in a civil and military view.—A lieutenant upon duty deſignedly quits his guard, and ſuffers it to be

* A few of them were confined.

drawn out by another officer, for a purpoſe, which he well knew (as we may collect from an appearance of caution, which only makes his behaviour the more criminal) to be in the higheſt degree illegal. Has this gentleman been called to a court martial to anſwer for his conduct? No. Has it been cenſured? No. Has it been in any ſhape inquired into? No.—Another lieutenant, not upon duty, nor even in his regimentals, is daring enough to order out the king's guard, over which he had properly no command, and engages them in a violation of the laws of his country, perhaps the moſt ſingular and extravagant that ever was attempted.—What puniſhment has *he* ſuffered? Literally none. Suppoſing he ſhould be proſecuted at common law for the reſcue, will that circumſtance, from which the miniſtry can derive no merit, excuſe or juſtify their ſuffering ſo flagrant a breach of military diſcipline to paſs by unpuniſhed, and unnoticed? Are they aware of the outrage offered to their ſovereign, when his own proper guard is ordered out to ſtop by main force, the execution of his laws? What are we to conclude from ſo ſcandalous a neglect of their duty, but

but that they have other views, which can only be anſwered by ſecuring the attachment of the guards? The miniſter would hardly be ſo cautious of offending them, if he did not mean, in due time, to call for their aſſiſtance.

WITH reſpect to the parties themſelves, let it be obſerved, that theſe gentlemen are neither young officers, nor very young men. Had they belonged to the unfledged race of enſigns, who infeſt our ſtreets, and diſhonor our public places, it might perhaps be ſufficient to ſend them back to that diſcipline, from which their parents, judging lightly from the maturity of their vices, had removed them too ſoon. In this caſe, I am ſorry to ſee, not ſo much the folly of youth, as the ſpirit of the corps, and the connivance of government. I do not queſtion that there are many brave and worthy officers in the regiments of guards. But conſidering them as a corps, I fear, it will be found that they are neither good ſoldiers, nor good ſubjects. Far be it from me to inſinuate the moſt diſtant reflection upon the army. On the contrary, I honour and eſteem the profeſſion;

and if theſe gentlemen were better ſoldiers, I am ſure they would be better ſubjects. It is not that there is any internal vice or defect in the profeſſion itſelf, as regulated in this country, but that it is the ſpirit of this particular corps, to deſpiſe their profeſſion, and that while they vainly aſſume the lead of the army, they make it matter of impertinent compariſon and triumph over the braveſt troops in the world (I mean our marching regiments) that *they* indeed ſtand upon higher ground, and are privileged to neglect the laborious forms of military diſcipline and duty. Without dwelling longer upon a moſt invidious ſubject, I ſhall leave it to military men, who have ſeen a ſervice more active than the parade, to determine whether or no I ſpeak truth.

How far this dangerous ſpirit has been encouraged by government, and to what pernicious purpoſes it may be applied hereafter, well deſerves our moſt ſerious conſideration. I know indeed, that when this affair happened, an affectation of alarm ran through the miniſtry. Something muſt be done to ſave appearances. The caſe was too flagrant to be

paſſed

paſſed by abſolutely without notice. But how have they acted? Inſtead of ordering the officers concerned, (and who, ſtrictly ſpeaking, are alone guilty,) to be put under arreſt, and brought to trial, they would have it underſtood, that they did their duty completely, in confining a ſerjeant and four private ſoldiers, until they ſhould be demanded by the civil power; ſo that while the officers, who ordered or permitted the thing to be done, eſcape without cenſure, the poor men who obeyed thoſe orders, who in a military view are no way reſponſible for what they did, and who for that reaſon have been diſcharged by the civil magiſtrates, are the only objects whom the miniſtry have thought proper to expoſe to puniſhment. They did not venture to bring even theſe men to a court martial, becauſe they knew their evidence would be fatal to ſome perſons, whom they were determined to protect. Otherwiſe, I doubt not, the lives of theſe unhappy, friendleſs ſoldiers would long ſince have been ſacrificed without ſcruple to the ſecurity of their guilty officers.

I HAVE been accuſed of endeavouring to enflame the paſſions of the people.—Let me now

now appeal to their underſtanding. If there be any tool of adminiſtration daring enough to deny theſe facts, or ſhameleſs enough to defend the conduct of the miniſtry, let him come forward. I care not under what title he appears. He ſhall find me ready to maintain the truth of my narrative, and the juſtice of my obſervations upon it, at the hazard of my utmoſt credit with the public.

UNDER the moſt arbitrary governments, the common adminiſtration of juſtice is ſuffered to take its courſe. The ſubject, though robbed of his ſhare in the legiſlature, is ſtill protected by the laws. The political freedom of the Engliſh conſtitution was once the pride and honour of an Engliſhman. The civil equality of the laws preſerved the property, and defended the ſafety of the ſubject. Are theſe glorious privileges the birthright of the people, or are we only tenants at the will of the miniſtry?—But that I know there is a ſpirit of reſiſtance in the hearts of my countrymen, that they value life, not by its conveniences, but by the independance and dignity of their condition, I ſhould, at this moment, appeal only to their diſcretion.

I ſhould perſuade them to baniſh from their minds all memory of what we were; I ſhould tell them this is not a time to remember that we were Engliſhmen; and give it as my laſt advice, to make ſome early agreement with the miniſter, that ſince it has pleaſed him to rob us of thoſe political rights, which once diſtinguiſhed the inhabitants of a country, where honour was happineſs, he would leave us at leaſt the humble, obedient ſecurity of citizens, and graciouſly condeſcend to protect us in our ſubmiſſion.

JUNIUS.

LETTER XXXI.

TO THE PRINTER OF THE PUBLIC ADVERTISER.

SIR, *November* 14, 1769.

THE variety of remarks, which have been made upon the laſt letter of *Junius*, and my own opinion of the Writer, who, whatever may be his faults, is certainly not a weak man, have induced me to examine, with ſome attention, the ſubject of that letter. I could not perſuade myſelf that, while he had plenty of important materials,

terials, he would have taken up a light or trifling occasion to attack the Ministry; much less could I conceive that it was his intention to ruin the officers concern'd in the rescue of general Gansel, or to injure the general himself. These are little objects, and can no way contribute to the great purposes he seems to have in view by addressing himself to the publick.—Without considering the ornamented stile he has adopted, I determined to look farther into the matter, before I decided upon the merits of his letter. The first step I took was to enquire into the truth of the facts; for if these were either false or misrepresented, the most artful exertion of his understanding, in reasoning upon them, would only be a disgrace to him.—Now, Sir, I have found every circumstance stated by *Junius* to be literally true. General Gansel persuaded the bailiffs to conduct him to the parade, and certainly solicited a Corporal and other Soldiers to assist him in making his escape. Captain Dodd did certainly apply to Captain Garth for the assistance of his guard. Captain Garth declined appearing himself, but stood aloof, while the other took upon him to order out the King's guard, and by

main

main force reſcued the General. It is alſo ſtrictly true, that the General was eſcorted by a file of muſqueteers to a place of ſecurity. —Theſe are facts, Mr. Woodfall, which I promiſe you no gentleman in the guards will deny. If all or any of them are falſe, why are they not contradicted by the parties themſelves? However ſecure againſt military cenſure, they have yet a character to loſe, and ſurely, if they are innocent, it is not beneath them to pay ſome attention to the opinion of the public.

The force of *Junius*'s Obſervations upon theſe facts cannot be better marked, than by ſtating and refuting the objections which have been made to them. One writer ſays, "Admitting the officers have offended, they "are puniſhable at common law, and will "you have a Britiſh ſubject puniſhed twice "for the ſame offence?"—I anſwer that they have committed two offences, both very enormous, and violated two laws. The reſcue is one offence, the flagrant breach of diſcipline another, and hitherto it does not appear that they have been puniſhed, or even cenſured for either. Another gentleman

lays

lays much ſtreſs upon the calamity of the caſe, and, inſtead of diſproving facts, appeals at once to the compaſſion of the public. This idea, as well as the inſinuation *that depriving the parties of their commiſſions would be an injury to their creditors*, can only refer to General Ganſel. The other officers are in no diſtreſs, therefore, have no claim to compaſſion, nor does it appear, that their creditors, if they have any, are more likely to be ſatisfied by their continuing in the guards. But this ſort of plea will not hold in any ſhape. Compaſſion to an offender, who has groſsly violated the laws, is in effect a cruelty to the peaceable ſubject who has obſerved them; and, even admitting the force of any alleviating circumſtances, it is nevertheleſs true, that, in this inſtance, the royal compaſſion has interpoſed too ſoon. The legal and proper mercy of a King of England may remit the puniſhment, but ought not to ſtop the trial.

Besides theſe particular objections, there has been a cry raiſed againſt *Junius* for his malice and injuſtice in attacking the miniſtry upon an event, which they could neither hinder

hinder nor foresee. This, I must affirm, is a false representation of his argument. He lays no stress upon the event itself, as a ground of accusation against the ministry, but dwells entirely upon their subsequent conduct. He does not say that they are answerable for the offence, but for the scandalous neglect of their duty, in suffering an offence, so flagrant, to pass by without notice or inquiry. Supposing them ever so regardless of what they owe to the public, and as indifferent about the opinion as they are about the interests of their country, what answer, as officers of the crown, will they give to *Junius*, when he asks them, *Are they aware of the outrage offered to their Sovereign, when his own proper guard is ordered out to stop, by main force, the execution of his laws?*—And when we see a ministry giving such a strange unaccountable protection to the officers of the guards, is it unfair to suspect, that they have some secret and unwarrantable motives for their conduct? If they feel themselves injured by such a suspicion, why do they not immediately clear themselves from it, by doing their duty? For the honour of the guards, I cannot help expressing another suspicion,

picion, that, if the commanding officer had not received a ſecret injunction to the contrary, he would, in the ordinary courſe of his buſineſs, have applied for a court martial to try the two ſubalterns; the one for quitting his guard;—the other for taking upon him the command of the guard, and employing it in the manner he did. I do not mean to enter into or defend the ſeverity, with which *Junius* treats the guards. On the contrary, I will ſuppoſe, for a moment, that they deſerve a very different character. If this be true, in what light will they conſider the conduct of the two ſubalterns, but as a general reproach and diſgrace to the whole corps? And will they not wiſh to ſee them cenſured in a military way, if it were only for the credit and diſcipline of the Regiment.

UPON the whole, Sir, the Miniſtry ſeem to me to have taken a very improper advantage of the good-nature of the public, whoſe humanity, they found, conſidered nothing in this affair but the diſtreſs of General Ganſel. They would perſuade us that it was only a common reſcue by a few diſorderly ſoldiers, and not the formal deliberate act

of

of the king's guard, headed by an officer, and the public has fallen into the deception. I think, therefore, we are obliged to *Junius* for the care he has taken to inquire into the facts, and for the juſt commentary with which he has given them to the world.—For my own part, I am as unwilling as any man to load the unfortunate; but, really, Sir, the precedent, with reſpect to the guards, is of a moſt important nature, and alarming enough (conſidering the conſequences with which it may be attended) to deſerve a parliamentary inquiry: when the guards are daring enough, not only to violate their own diſcipline, but publicly and with the moſt atrocious violence to ſtop the execution of the laws, and when ſuch extraordinary offences paſs with impunity, believe me, Sir, the precedent ſtrikes deep.

PHILO JUNIUS.

LETTER XXXII.

TO THE PRINTER OF THE PUBLIC ADVERTISER.

SIR, 15. *Nov.* 1769.

I ADMIT the claim of a gentleman, who publishes in the Gazetteer under the name of *Modestus*. He has some right to expect an answer from me; though, I think, not so much from the merit or importance of his objections, as from my own voluntary engagement. I had a reason for not taking notice of him sooner, which, as he is a candid person, I believe he will think sufficient. In my first letter, I took for granted, from the time which had elapsed, that there was no intention to censure, nor even to try the persons concerned in the rescue of General Gansel; but *Modestus* having since either affirmed, or strongly insinuated, that the offenders might still be brought to a legal trial, any attempt to prejudge the cause, or to prejudice the minds of a jury, or a court martial, would be highly improper.

A MAN, more hostile to the ministry than I am, would not so often remind them of their

their duty. If the Duke of Grafton will not perform the duty of his ſtation, why is he miniſter?—I will not deſcend to a ſcurrilous altercation with any man: but this is a ſubject too important to be paſſed over with ſilent indifference. If the gentlemen, whoſe conduct is in queſtion, are not brought to a trial, the Duke of Grafton ſhall hear from me again.

THE motives on which I am ſuppoſed to have taken up this cauſe, are of little importance, compared with the facts themſelves, and the obſervations I have made upon them. Without a vain profeſſion of integrity, which, in theſe times might juſtly be ſuſpected, I ſhall ſhew myſelf in effect a friend to the intereſts of my countrymen, and leave it to them to determine, whether I am moved by a perſonal malevolence to three private gentlemen, or merely by a hope of perplexing the miniſtry, or whether I am animated by a juſt and honourable purpoſe of obtaining a ſatiſfaction to the laws of this country, equal, if poſſible, to the violation they have ſuffered.

JUNIUS.

LETTER XXXIII.

TO HIS GRACE THE DUKE OF GRAFTON.

MY LORD, 29. *Nov.* 1769.

THOUGH my opinion of your Grace's integrity was but little affected by the coyneſs with which you received Mr. Vaughan's propoſals, I confeſs I give you ſome credit for your diſcretion. You had a fair opportunity of diſplaying a certain delicacy, of which you had not been ſuſpected; and you were in the right to make uſe of it. By laying in a moderate ſtock of reputation, you undoubtedly meant to provide for the future neceſſities of your character, that with an honourable reſiſtance upon record, you might ſafely indulge your genius, and yield to a favourite inclination with ſecurity. But you have diſcovered your purpoſes too ſoon; and, inſtead of the modeſt reſerve of virtue, have ſhewn us the termagant chaſtity of a prude, who gratifies her paſſions with diſtinction, and proſecutes one lover for a rape, while ſhe ſolicits the lewd embraces of another.

YOUR

YOUR cheek turns pale; for a guilty conſcience tells you, you are undone.—Come forward, thou virtuous miniſter, and tell the world by what intereſt Mr. Hine has been recommended to ſo extraordinary a mark of his Majeſty's favour; what was the price of the patent he has bought, and to what honourable purpoſe the purchaſe money has been applied. Nothing leſs than many thouſands could pay Colonel Burgoyne's expences at Preſton. Do you dare to proſecute ſuch a creature as Vaughan, while you are baſely ſetting up the Royal Patronage to auction? Do you dare to complain of an attack upon your own honour, while you are ſelling the favours of the crown, to raiſe a fund for corrupting the morals of the people? And, do you think it poſſible ſuch enormities ſhould eſcape without impeachment? It is indeed highly your intereſt to maintain the preſent houſe of commons. Having ſold the nation to you in groſs, they will undoubtedly protect you in the detail; for while they patronize your crimes, they feel for their own.

JUNIUS.

LETTER XXXIV.

TO HIS GRACE THE DUKE OF GRAFTON.

MY LORD, 12. *Dec.* 1769.

I FIND with ſome ſurpriſe, that you are not ſupported as you deſerve. Your moſt determined advocates have ſcruples about them, which you are unacquainted with; and, though there be nothing too hazardous for your Grace to engage in, there are ſome things too infamous for the vileſt proſtitute of a news-paper to defend *. In what other manner ſhall we account for the profound, ſubmiſſive ſilence, which you and your friends have obſerved upon a charge, which called immediately for the cleareſt refutation, and would have juſtified the ſevereſt meaſures of reſentment? I did not attempt to blaſt your character by an indirect, ambiguous inſinuation, but candidly ſtated

* From the publication of the preceding to this date, not one word was ſaid in defence of the infamous Duke of Grafton. But vice and impudence ſoon recovered themſelves, and the ſale of the royal favour was openly avowed and defended. We acknowledge the piety of St. James's; but what is become of *his* morality?

to

to you a plain fact, which struck directly at the integrity of a privy counsellor, of a first commissioner of the treasury, and of a leading minister, who is supposed to enjoy the first share in his Majesty's confidence *. In every one of these capacities I employed the most moderate terms to charge you with treachery to your Sovereign, and breach of trust in your office. I accused you of having sold a patent place in the collection of the customs at Exeter, to one Mr. Hine, who, unable or unwilling to deposit the whole purchase-money himself, raised part of it by contribution, and has now a certain Doctor Brooke quartered upon the salary for one hundred pounds a year.—No sale by the candle was ever conducted with greater formality.—I affirm that the price, at which the place was knocked down (and which, I have good reason to think, was not less than three thousand five hundred pounds) was, with your connivance and consent, paid to Colonel Burgoyne, to reward him, I presume, for the decency of his deportment at Preston; or to reimburse him, perhaps, for the fine of one thousand pounds, which, for that very de-

* And by the same means preserves it to this hour.

portment, the court of King's Bench thought proper to ſet upon him.—It is not often that the chief juſtice and the prime miniſter are ſo ſtrangely at variance in their opinions of men and things.

I THANK God there is not in human nature a degree of impudence daring enough to deny the charge I have fixed upon you. * Your courteous ſecretary, your confidential architect †, are ſilent as the grave. Even Mr. Rigby's countenance fails him. He violates his ſecond nature, and bluſhes whenever he ſpeaks of you.—Perhaps the noble Colonel himſelf will relieve you. No man is more tender of his reputation. He is not only nice, but perfectly ſore in every thing that touches his honour. If any man, for example, were to accuſe him of taking his ſtand at a gaming-table, and watching, with the ſobereſt attention, for a fair opportunity of engaging a drunken young nobleman at piquet, he would undoubtedly conſider it as an infamous aſperſion upon his character,

* Tommy Bradſhaw.

† Mr. Taylor. He and George Roſs, (the Scotch agent and worthy confidante of Lord Mansfield) managed the buſineſs.

and

and resent it like a man of honour.—Acquitting him therefore of drawing a regular and splendid subsistence from any unworthy practices, either in his own house or elsewhere, let me ask your Grace, for what military merits you have been pleased to reward him with military government? He had a regiment of dragoons, which one would imagine, was at least an equivalent for any services he ever performed. Besides, he is but a young officer considering his preferment, and, except in his activity at Preston, not very conspicuous in his profession. But it seems, the sale of a civil employment was not sufficient, and military governments, which were intended for the support of worn out veterans, must be thrown into the scale, to defray the extensive bribery of a contested election. Are these the steps you take to secure to your Sovereign the attachment of his army? With what countenance dare you appear in the royal presence, branded as you are with the infamy of a notorious breach of trust? With what countenance can you take your seat at the treasury-board or in council, when you feel that every circulating whisper is at your expence alone, and stabs you to the heart? Have you a single friend in parlia-

ment

ment so shameless, so thoroughly abandoned, as to undertake your defence? You know, my Lord, that there is not a man in either house, whose character, however flagitious, would not be ruined by mixing his reputation with yours; and does not your heart inform you, that you are degraded below the condition of a man, when you are obliged to hear these insults with submission, and even to thank me for my moderation?

We are told, by the highest judicial authority, that Mr. Vaughan's offer to purchase the reversion of a patent in Jamaica (which he was otherwise sufficiently entitled to) amounted to a high misdemeanour. Be it so: and if he deserves it, let him be punished. But the learned judge might have had a fairer opportunity of displaying the powers of his eloquence. Having delivered himself with so much energy upon the criminal nature, and dangerous consequences of any attempt to corrupt a man in your Grace's station, what would he have said to the minister himself, to that very privy counsellor, to that first commissioner of the treasury, who does not wait for, but impatiently solicits the touch of corruption; who employs the meanest

meaneſt of his creatures in theſe honourable ſervices, and, forgetting the genius and fidelity of his ſecretary, deſcends to apply to his houſe-builder for aſſiſtance?

THIS affair, my Lord, will do infinite credit to government, if, to clear your character, you ſhould think proper to bring it into the houſe of Lords, or into the court of King's Bench.——But, my Lord, you dare not do either.

JUNIUS.

A little before the publication of this and the preceding letter, the chaſte Duke of Grafton had commenced a proſecution againſt Mr. Samuel Vaughan, for endeavouring to corrupt his integrity by an office of five thouſand pounds for a patent place in Jamaica. A rule to ſhew cauſe, why an information ſhould not be exhibited againſt Vaughan for certain miſdemeanors, being granted by the Court of King's Bench, the matter was ſolemnly argued on the 27. of November, 1769, and, by the unanimous opinion of the four judges, the rule was made abſolute. The pleadings and ſpeeches were accurately taken in ſhort-hand and publiſhed. The whole of Lord Mansfield's ſpeech, and particularly the following extracts from it, deſerve the reader's attention. "A practice "of the kind complained of here is certainly diſhonourable "and ſcandalous.---If a man, ſtanding under the relation of "an officer under the King, or of a perſon in whom the King "puts confidence, or of a miniſter, takes money for the uſe "of that confidence the King puts in him, he baſely betrays "the King,---he baſely betrays his truſt.----If the King ſo'd "the office, it would be acting contrary to the truſt the con-"ſtitution hath repoſed in him. The conſtitution does not

"in-

" intend the crown should sell those offices, to raise a revenue
" out of them.---Is it possible to hesitate, whether this would
" not be criminal in the Duke of Grafton;---contrary to his
" duty as a privy councillor;---contrary to his duty as a mi-
" nister---contrary to his duty as a subject.----His advice
" should be free according to his judgement;---It is the duty
" of his office;---he has sworn to it."---Notwithstanding all
this, the chaste Duke of Grafton certainly sold a patent place
to Mr. Hine for three thousand five hundred pounds; and,
for so doing, is now Lord Privy Seal to the chaste George,
with whose piety we are perpetually deafened. If the house
of commons had done their duty, and impeached the black
Duke for this most infamous breach of trust, how woefully
must poor, honest Mansfield have been puzzled! His em-
barassment would have afforded the most ridiculous scene, that
ever was exhibited. To save the worthy judge from this perplexity, and the no less worthy Duke from impeachment, the
prosecution against *Vaughan* was, immediately dropped upon
my discovery and publication of the Duke's treachery. The
suffering this charge to pass, without any inquiry, fixes
shameless prostitution upon the face of the house of commons, more strongly than even the Middlesex election.----
Yet the licentiousness of the press is complained of!

LET-

LETTER XXXV.

TO THE PRINTER OF THE PUBLIC ADVERTISER.

19. December, 1769.

When the complaints of a brave and powerful people are obſerved to encreaſe in proportion to the wrongs they have ſuffered; when, inſtead of ſinking into ſubmiſſion, they are rouſed to reſiſtance, the time will ſoon arrive at which every inferior conſideration muſt yield to the ſecurity of the Sovereign, and to the general ſafety of the ſtate. There is a moment of difficulty and danger, at which flattery and falſhood can no longer deceive, and ſimplicity itſelf can no longer be miſled. Let us ſuppoſe it arrived. Let us ſuppoſe a gracious, well-intentioned prince, made ſenſible at laſt of the great duty he owes to his people, and of his own diſgraceful ſituation; that he looks round him for aſſiſtance, and aſks for no advice, but how to gratify the wiſhes, and ſecure the happineſs of his ſubjects. In theſe circumſtances, it may be matter of curious

curious SPECULATION to consider, if an honest man were permitted to approach a King, in what terms he would address himself to his Sovereign. Let it be imagined, no matter how improbable, that the first prejudice against his character is removed, that the ceremonious difficulties of an audience are surmounted, that he feels himself animated by the purest and most honourable affections to his King and country, and that the great person, whom he addresses, has spirit enough to bid him speak freely, and understanding enough to listen to him with attention. Unacquainted with the vain impertinence of forms, he would deliver his sentiments with dignity and firmness, but not without respect.

SIR,

IT is the misfortune of your life, and originally the cause of every reproach and distress, which has attended your government, that you should never have been acquainted with the language of truth, until you heard it in the complaints of your people. It is not, however, too late to correct the error of your education. We are still inclined to make an indulgent allowance for the pernicious

nicious lessons you received in your youth, and to form the most sanguine hopes from the natural benevolence of your disposition *. We are far from thinking you capable of a direct, deliberate purpose to invade those original rights of your subjects, on which all their civil and political liberties depend. Had it been possible for us to entertain a suspicion so dishonourable to your character, we should

* The plan of tutelage and future dominion over the heir apparent, laid many years ago at Carlton-house between the Princess Dowager and her favourite the Earl of Bute, was as gross and palpable, as that, which was concerted between Anne of Austria and Cardinal Mazarin, to govern Lewis the Fourteenth, and in effect to prolong his minority until the end of their lives. That prince had strong natural parts, and used frequently to blush for his own ignorance and want of education, which had been wilfully neglected by his mother and her minion. A little experience however soon shewed him how shamefully he had been treated, and for what infamous purposes he had been kept in ignorance. Our great Edward too, at an early period, had sense enough to understand the nature of the connection between his abandoned mother, and the detested Mortimer. But, since that time, human nature, we may observe, is greatly altered for the better Dowagers may be chaste, and minions may be honest. When it was proposed to settle the present King's household as Prince of Wales, it is well known that the Earl of Bute was forced into it, in direct contradiction to the late King's inclination. *That* was the salient point, from which all the mischiefs and disgraces of the present reign, took life and motion. From that moment, Lord Bute never suffered the Prince of Wales to be an instant out of his sight.---We need not look farther.

long

long ſince have adopted a ſtyle of remonſtrance very diſtant from the humility of complaint. The doctrine inculcated by our laws, *That the King can do no wrong*, is admitted without reluctance. We ſeparate the amiable, good-natured prince from the folly and treachery of his ſervants, and the private virtues of the man from the vices of his government. Were it not for this juſt diſtinction, I know not whether your Majeſty's condition, or that of the Engliſh nation, would deſerve moſt to be lamented. I would prepare your mind for a favourable reception of truth, by removing every painful, offenſive idea of perſonal reproach. Your ſubjects, Sir, wiſh for nothing but that, as *they* are reaſonable and affectionate enough to ſeparate your perſon from your government, ſo *you*, in your turn, ſhould diſtinguiſh between the conduct, which becomes the permanent dignity of a King, and that which ſerves only to promote the temporary intereſt and miſerable ambition of a miniſter.

You aſcended the throne with a declared, and, I doubt not, a ſincere reſolution of giving univerſal ſatisfaction to your ſubjects. You found them pleaſed with the novelty of a young prince, whoſe countenance promiſed

even

even more than his words, and loyal to you not only from principle, but paſſion. It was not a cold profeſſion of allegiance to the firſt magiſtrate, but a partial, animated attachment to a favourite prince, the native of their country. They did not wait to examine your conduct, nor to be determined by experience, but gave you a generous credit for the future bleſſings of your reign, and paid you in advance the deareſt tribute of their affections. Such, Sir, was once the diſpoſition of a people, who now ſurround your throne with reproaches and complaints. Do juſtice to yourſelf. Baniſh from your mind thoſe unworthy opinions, with which ſome intereſted perſons have laboured to poſſeſs you. Diſtruſt the men, who tell you that the Engliſh are naturally light and inconſtant; —that they complain without a cauſe. Withdraw your confidence equally from all parties: from miniſters, favourites, and relations; and let there be one moment in your life, in which you have conſulted your own underſtanding.

WHEN you affectedly renounced the name of Engliſhman, believe me, Sir, you were perſuaded to pay a very ill-judged compliment to one part of your ſubjects, at the expence of another. While the natives of Scotland are not in actual rebellion, they are undoubtedly intitled to protection; nor do I mean to condemn the policy of giving ſome encouragement to the novelty of their affections for the houſe of Hanover. I am ready to hope for every thing from their new-born zeal, and from the future ſteadineſs of their allegiance. But hitherto they have no claim to your favour. To honour them with a determined predilection and confidence, in excluſion of your Engliſh ſubjects, who placed your family, and in ſpite of treachery and rebellion, have ſupported it upon the throne, is a miſtake too groſs, even for the unſuſpecting generoſity of youth. In this error we ſee a capital violation of the moſt obvious rules of policy and prudence. We trace it, however, to an original bias in your education, and are ready to allow for your inexperience.

To the ſame early influence we attribute it, that you have deſcended to take a ſhare not only in the narrow views and intereſts of particular perſons, but in the fatal malignity of their paſſions. At your acceſſion to the throne, the whole ſyſtem of government was altered, not from wiſdom or deliberation, but becauſe it had been adopted by your predeceſſor. A little perſonal motive of pique and reſentment was ſufficient to remove the ableſt ſervants of the crown *; but it is not in this country, Sir, that ſuch men can be diſhonoured by the frowns of a King. They were diſmiſſed, but could not be diſgraced. Without entering into a minuter diſcuſſion of the merits of the peace, we may obſerve, in the imprudent hurry with which the firſt overtures from France were accepted, in the conduct of the negotiation, and terms of the treaty, the ſtrongeſt marks of that precipitate ſpirit of conceſſion, with which a certain part of your ſubjects have been at all times ready to purchaſe a peace with the natural enemies of this country. On *your* part we are ſatiſfied that every thing was honourable and ſincere, and if England was ſold to France, we doubt not that your Majeſty was equally betrayed. The conditions of the peace were matter of grief and ſurpriſe to your ſubjects,

* One of the firſt acts of the preſent reign was to diſmiſs Mr. Legge, becauſe he had ſome years before refuſed to yield his intereſt in Hampſhire to a Scotchman recommended by Lord Bute. This was the reaſon publicly aſſigned by his Lordſhip.

But not the immediate cauſe of their preſent diſcontent.

HITHERTO, Sir, you had been ſacrificed to the prejudices and paſſions of others. With what firmneſs will you bear the mention of your own?

A MAN, not very honourably diſtinguiſhed in the world, commences a formal attack upon your favourite, conſidering nothing, but how he might beſt expoſe his perſon and principles to deteſtation, and the national character of his countrymen to contempt. The natives of that country, Sir, are as much diſtinguiſhed by a peculiar character, as by your Majeſty's favour. Like another choſen people, they have been conducted into the land of plenty, where they find themſelves effectually marked, and divided from mankind. There is hardly a period, at which the moſt irregular character may not be redeemed. The miſtakes of one ſex find a retreat in patriotiſm; thoſe of the other in devotion. Mr. Wilkes brought with him into politics the ſame liberal ſentiments, by which his private conduct had been directed, and ſeemed to think, that, as there are few exceſſes, in which

which an English gentleman may not be permitted to indulge, the same latitude was allowed him in the choice of his political principles, and in the spirit of maintaining them.—I mean to state, not entirely to defend his conduct. In the earnestness of his zeal, he suffered some unwarrantable insinuations to escape him. He said more than moderate men would justify; but not enough to entitle him to the honour of your Majesty's personal resentment. The rays of Royal indignation, collected upon him, served only to illuminate, and could not consume. Animated by the favour of the people on one side, and heated by persecution on the other, his views and sentiments changed with his situation. Hardly serious at first, he is now an enthusiast. The coldest bodies warm with opposition, the hardest sparkle in collision. There is a holy mistaken zeal in politics as well as religion. By persuading others, we convince ourselves. The passions are engaged, and create a maternal affection in the mind, which forces us to love the cause, for which we suffer.—Is this a contention worthy of a King? Are you not sensible how much the meanness of the cause gives an air of ridicule to the serious difficulties into which you have been betrayed? the deſtruction of one man has been now, for many years, the ſole object of your government, and if there can be any thing ſtill more diſgraceful, we have ſeen, for ſuch an object, the utmoſt influence of the executive power, and every miniſterial artifice exerted without ſucceſs. Nor can you ever ſucceed, unleſs *he* ſhould be imprudent enough to forfeit the protection of thoſe laws, to which you owe your crown, or unleſs your miniſters ſhould perſuade you to make it a queſtion of force alone, and try the whole ſtrength of government in oppoſition to the people. The leſſons *he* has received from experience, will probably guard him from ſuch exceſs of folly; and in your Majeſty's virtues we find an unqueſtionable aſſurance that no illegal violence will be attempted.

FAR from ſuſpecting you of ſo horrible a deſign, we would attribute the continued violation of the laws, and even this laſt enormous attack upon the vital principles of the conſtitution, to an ill-adviſed, unworthy, perſonal reſentment. From one falſe ſtep you have been betrayed into another, and as the cauſe was unworthy of you, your miniſters were

were determined that the prudence of the execution ſhould correſpond with the wiſdom and dignity of the deſign. They have reduced you to the neceſſity of chooſing out of a variety of difficulties;—to a ſituation ſo unhappy, that you can neither do wrong without ruin, nor right without affliction. Theſe worthy ſervants have undoubtedly given you many ſingular proofs of their abilities. Not contented with making Mr. Wilkes a man of importance, they have judiciouſly transferred the queſtion, from the rihts and intereſts of one man, to the moſt important rights and intereſts of the people, and forced your ſubjects, from wiſhing well to the cauſe of an individual, to unite with him in their own. Let them proceed as they have begun, and your Majeſty need not doubt that the cataſtrophe will do no diſhonour to the conduct of the piece.

THE circumſtances to which you are reduced, will not admit of a compromiſe with the Engliſh nation. Undeciſive, qualifying meaſures will diſgrace your government ſtill more than open violence, and, without ſatiſfying the people, will excite their contempt.

They have too much underſtanding and ſpirit to accept of an indirect ſatisfaction for a direct injury. Nothing leſs than a repeal, as formal as the reſolution itſelf, can heal the wound, which has been given to the conſtitution, nor will any thing leſs be accepted. I can readily believe that there is an influence ſufficient to recal that pernicious vote. The houſe of commons undoubtedly conſider their duty to the crown as paramont to all other obligations. To *us* they are only indebted for an accidental exiſtence, and have juſtly transferred their gratitude from their parents to their benefactors;—from thoſe, who gave them birth, to the miniſter, from whoſe benevolence they derive the comforts and pleaſures of their political life;—who has taken the tendereſt care of their infancy, and relieves their neceſſities without offending their delicacy. But, if it were poſſible for their integrity to be degraded to a condition ſo vile and abject, that, compared with it, the preſent eſtimation they ſtand in is a ſtate of honour and reſpect, conſider, Sir, in what manner you will afterwards proceed. Can you conceive that the peeple of this country will long ſubmit to be governed by ſo flexible a houſe of commons! It is not in the nature

of

of human society, that any form of government, in such circumstances, can long be preserved. In ours, the general contempt of the people is as fatal as their detestation. Such, I am persuaded, would be the necessary effect of any base concession made by the present house of commons, and, as a qualifying measure would not be accepted, it remains for you to decide whether you will, at any hazard, support a set of men, who have reduced you to this unhappy dilemma, or whether you will gratify the united wishes of the whole people of England by dissolving the parliament.

TAKING it for granted, as I do very sincerely, that you have personally no design against the constitution, nor any view inconsistent with the good of your subjects, I think you cannot hesitate long upon the choice, which it equally concerns your interest, and your honour to adopt. On one side, you hazard the affections of all your English subjects; you relinquish every hope of repose to yourself, and you endanger the establishment of your family for ever. All this you venture for no object whatsoever, or for such an ob-

object, as it would be an affront to you to name. Men of sense will examine your conduct with suspicion; while those who are incapable of comprehending to what degree they are injured, afflict you with clamours equally insolent and unmeaning. Supposing it possible that no fatal struggle should ensue, you determine at once to be unhappy, without the hope of a compensation either from interest or ambition. If an English King be hated or despised, he *must* be unhappy; and this perhaps is the only political truth, which he ought to be convinced of without experiment. But if the English people should no longer confine their resentment to a submissive representation of their wrongs; if, following the glorious example of their ancestors, they should no longer appeal to the creature of the constitution, but to that high Being, who gave them the rights of humanity, whose gifts it were sacrilege to surrender, let me ask you, Sir, upon what part of your subjects would you rely for assistance?

THE people of Ireland have been uniformly plundered and oppressed. In return, they give

give you every day fresh marks of their resentment. They despise the miserable governor you have sent them *, because he is the creature of Lord Bute; nor is it from any natural confusion in their ideas, that they are so ready to confound the original of a King with the disgraceful representation of him.

THE distance of the Colonies would make it impossible for them to take an active concern in your affairs, if they were as well affected to your government as they once pretended to be to your person. They were ready enough to distinguish between *you* and your ministers. They complained of an act of the legislature, but traced the origin of it no higher than to the servants of the crown: They pleased themselves with the hope that their Sovereign, if not favourable to their cause, at least was impartial. The decisive, personal part you took against them, has effectually banished that first distinctiom from their minds †. They consider you as united

* Viscount Townshend, sent over on the plan of being resident governor. The history of his ridiculous administration shall not be lost to the public.

† In the King's speech of 8. November, 1768, it was declared "That the spirit of faction had broken out a fresh in "some

ted with your servants against America, and know how to distinguish the Sovereign and a venal parliament on one side, from the real sentiments of the English people on the other. Looking forward to independence, they might possibly receive you for their King; but, if ever you retire to America, be assured they will give you such a covenant to digest, as the presbytery of Scotland would have been ashamed to offer to Charles the second. They left their native land in search of freedom, and found it in a desart. Divided as they are into a thousand forms of policy and religion, there is one point in which they all agree:—they equally detest the pageantry of a King, and the supercilious hypocrisy of a bishop.

It is not then from the alienated affections of Ireland or America, that you can reasonably look for assistance; still less from the people of England, who are actually con-

"some of the colonies, and, in one of them, proceeded to acts "of violence and resistance to the execution of the laws;---- "that Boston was in a state of disobedience to all law and government, and had proceeded to measures subversive of the "constitution, and attended with circumstances, that manifested a disposition to throw off their dependance on Great "Britain."

tending

tending for their rights, and in this great queſtion, are parties againſt you. You are not however, deſtitute of every appearance of ſupport: You have all the Jacobites, Non-jurors, Roman Catholics, and Tories of this country, and all Scotland without exception. Conſidering from what family you are deſcended, the choice of your friends has been ſingularly directed; and truly, Sir, if you had not loſt the whig intereſt of England, I ſhould admire your dexterity in turning the hearts of your enemies. Is it poſſible for you to place any confidence in men, who, before they are faithful to you, muſt renounce every opinion, and betray every principle, both in church and ſtate, which they inherit from their anceſtors, and are confirmed in by their education? whoſe numbers are ſo inconſiderable, that they have long ſince been obliged to give up the principles and language which diſtinguiſh them as a party, and to fight under the banners of their enemies? Their zeal begins with hypocriſy, and muſt conclude in treachery. At firſt they deceive; at laſt they betray.

As to the Scotch, I muſt ſuppoſe your heart and underſtanding ſo biaſſed, from your earlieſt

lieſt infancy, in their favour, that nothing leſs than *your own* misfortunes can undeceive you. You will not accept of the uniform experience of your anceſtors; and when once a man is determined to believe, the very abſurdity of the doctrine confirms him in his faith. A bigoted underſtanding can draw a proof of attachment to the houſe of Hanover from a notorious zeal for the houſe of Stuart, and find an earneſt of future loyalty in former rebellions. Appearances are however in their favour; ſo ſtrongly indeed, that one would think they had forgotten that you are their lawful King, and had miſtaken you for a pretender to the crown. Let it be admitted then that the Scotch are as ſincere in their preſent profeſſions, as if you were in reality not an Engliſhman, but a Briton of the North. You would not be the firſt prince, of their native country, againſt whom they have rebelled, nor the firſt whom they have baſely betrayed. Have you forgotten, Sir, or has your favourite concealed from you that part of our hiſtory, when the unhappy Charles, (and he too had private virtues) fled from the open, avowed indignation of his Engliſh ſubjects, and ſurrendered himſelf at diſcretion to the good faith

faith of his own countrymen. Without looking for ſupport in their affections as ſubjects, he applied only to their honour as gentlemen, for protection. They received him as they would your Majeſty, with bows, and ſmiles, and falſhood, and kept him until they had ſettled their bargain with the Engliſh parliament; then baſely ſold their native king to the vengeance of his enemies. This, Sir, was not the act of a few traitors, but the deliberate treachery of a Scotch parliament, repreſenting the nation. A wiſe prince might draw from it two leſſons of equal utility to himſelf. On one ſide he might learn to dread the undiſguiſed reſentment of a generous people, who dare openly aſſert their rights, and who, in a juſt cauſe are ready to meet their Sovereign in the field. On the other ſide, he would be taught to apprehend ſomething far more formidable;—a fawning treachery, againſt which no prudence can guard, no courage can defend. The inſidious ſmile upon the cheek would warn him of the canker in the heart.

FROM the uſes, to which one part of the army has been too frequently applied, you

have

have ſome reaſon to expect, that there are no ſervices they would refuſe. Here too we trace the partiality of your underſtanding. You take the ſenſe of the army from the conduct of the guards, with the ſame juſtice with which you collect the ſenſe of the people from the repreſentations of the miniſtry. Your marching regiments, Sir, will not make the guards their example either as ſoldiers or ſubjects. They feel and reſent, as they ought to do, that invariable, undiſtinguiſhing favour with which the guards are treated; * while thoſe gallant troops, by whom every hazardous, every laborious ſervice is performed, are left to periſh in garriſons abroad, or pine in quarters at home, neglected and forgotten. If they had no ſenſe of the great original duty they owe their country, their reſentment would operate like patriotiſm,

* The number of commiſſioned officers in the guards are to the marching regiments as *one* to eleven;---the number of regiments given to the guards, compared with thoſe given to the line, is about three to one, at a moderate computation; conſequently the partiality in favour of the guards is as thirty-three to one.---So much for the officers.---The private men have four-pence a day to ſubſiſt on; and five hundred laſhes, if they deſert. Under this puniſhment, they frequently expire. With theſe encouragements, it is ſuppoſed, they may be depended upon, whenever a certain perſon thinks it neceſſary to butcher his *fellow ſubjects*.

and

and leave your cauſe to be defended by thoſe, to whom you have laviſhed the rewards and honours of their profeſſion. The Prætorian Bands, enervated and debauched as they were, had ſtill ſtrength enough to awe the Roman populace: but when the diſtant legions took the alarm, they marched to Rome, and gave away the empire.

On this ſide then, which ever way you turn your eyes, you ſee nothing but perplexity and diſtreſs. You may determine to ſupport the very miniſtry who have reduced your affairs to this deplorable ſituation: you may ſhelter yourſelf under the forms of a parliament, and ſet your people at defiance. But be aſſured, Sir, that ſuch a reſolution would be as imprudent as it would be odious. If it did not immediately ſhake your eſtabliſhment, it would rob you of your peace of mind for ever.

On the other, how different is the proſpect! How eaſy, how ſafe and honourable is the path before you! The Engliſh nation declare they are groſsly injured by their repreſentatives, and ſolicit your Majeſty to exert your lawful prerogative, and give them an an opportunity of recalling a truſt, which, they find, has been ſcandalouſly abuſed. You are not to be told that the power of the houſe of commons is not original, but delegated to them for the welfare of the people, from whom they received it. A queſtion of right ariſes between the conſtituent and the repreſentative body. By what authority ſhall it be decided? Will your Majeſty interfere in a queſtion in which you have properly no immediate concern.—It would be a ſtep equally odious and unneceſſary. Shall the lords be called upon to determine the rights and privileges of the commons?—They cannot do it without a flagrant breach of the conſtitution. Or will you refer it to the judges?—They have often told your anceſtors, that the law of parliament is above them. What party then remains, but to leave it to the people to determine for themſelves? They alone are injured; and ſince there is no ſuperior power, to which the cauſe can be referred, they alone ought to determine.

I DO not mean to perplex you with a tedious argument upon a ſubject already ſo diſcuſſed, that inſpiration could hardly throw a new light upon it. There are, however, two points of view, in which it particularly imports your Majeſty to conſider, the late proceedings of the houſe of commons. By depriving a ſubject of his birthright, they have attributed to their own vote an authority equal to an act of the whole legiſlature; and, tho' perhaps not with the ſame motives, have ſtrictly followed the example of the long parliament, which firſt declared the regal office uſeleſs, and ſoon after with as little ceremony, diſſolved the houſe of lords. The ſame pretended power, which robs an Engliſh ſubject of his birth-right, may rob an Engliſh King of his crown. In another view, the reſolution of the houſe of commons, apparently not ſo dangerous to your Majeſty, is ſtill more alarming to your people. Not contented with diveſting one man of his right, they have arbitrarily conveyed that right to another. They have ſet aſide a return as illegal, without daring to cenſure thoſe officers, who were particularly apprized of Mr. Wilkes's incapacity, not only by the declaration of the houſe, but expreſsly by the writ directed to them, and, who nevertheleſs returned him as duly elected. They have rejected the majority of votes, the only criterion, by which our laws judge of the sense of the people; they have transferred the right of election from the collective to the representative body; and by these acts, taken separately or together, they have essentially altered the original constitution of the house of commons. Versed, as your Majesty undoubtedly is, in the English history, it cannot easily escape you, how much it is your interest, as well as your duty to prevent one of the three estates from encroaching upon the province of the other two, or assuming the authority of them all. When once they have departed from the great constitutional line, by which all their proceedings should be directed, who will answer for their future moderation? Or what assurance will they give you, that, when they have trampled upon their equals, they will submit to a superior? Your Majesty may learn hereafter, how nearly the slave and tyrant are allied.

SOME of your council, more candid than the rest, admit the abandoned profligacy of the present house of commons, but oppose their dissolution upon an opinion, I confess not

not very unwarrantable that their successors, would be equally at the disposal of the treasury. I cannot persuade myself that the nation will have profited so little by experience. But if that opinion were well founded, you might then gratify our wishes at an easy rate, and appease the present clamour against your government, without offering any material injury to the favourite cause of corruption.

You have still an honourable part to act. The affections of your subjects may still be recovered. But before you subdue *their* hearts, you must gain a noble victory over your own. Discard those little, personal resentments, which have too long directed your public conduct. Pardon this man the remainder of his punishment, and if resentment still prevails, make it, what it should have been long since, an act, not of mercy, but contempt. He will soon fall back into his natural station, —a silent senator, and hardly supporting the weekly eloquence of a news paper. The gentle breath of peace would leave him on the surface, neglected and unremoved. It is only the tempest, that lifts him from his place.

WITHOUT consulting your minister, call together your whole council. Let it appear to the public that you can determine and act for yourself. Come forward to your people. Lay aside the wretched formalities of a King, and speak to your subjects with the spirit of a man, and in the language of a gentleman. Tell them you have been fatally deceived. The acknowledgement will be no disgrace, but rather an honour to your understanding. Tell them you are determined to remove every cause of complaint against your government; that you will give your confidence to no man, who does not possess the confidence of your subjects; and leave it to themselves to determine, by their conduct at a future election, whether or no it be in reality the general sense of the nation, that their rights have been arbitrarily invaded by the present house of commons, and the constitution betrayed. They will then do justice to their representatives and to themselves.

THESE sentiments, Sir, and the stile they are conveyed in, may be offensive, perhaps, because they are new to you. Accustomed to the language of courtiers, you measure their affections by the vehemence of their expressions;

ſions; and, when they only praiſe you indirectly, you admire their ſincerity. But this is not a time to trifle with your fortune. They deceive you, Sir, who tell you that you have many friends, whoſe affections are founded upon a principle of perſonal attachment. The firſt foundation of friendſhip is not the power of conferring benefits, but the equality with which they are received, and *may* be returned. The fortune, which made you a King, forbad you to have a friend. It is a law of nature which cannot be violated with impunity. The miſtaken prince, who looks for friendſhip, will find a favourite, and in that favourite the ruin of his affairs.

THE people of England are loyal to the houſe of Hanover, not from a vain preference of one family to another, but from a conviction that the eſtabliſhment of that family was neceſſary to the ſupport of their civil and religious liberties. This, Sir, is a principle of allegiance equally ſolid and rational;—fit for Engliſhmen to adopt, and well worthy of your Majeſty's encouragement. We cannot long be deluded by nominal diſtinctions. The name of Stuart, of itſelf, is only contemptible;—armed with the Sovereign authority, their principles are formidable. The Prince, who imitates their conduct, should be warned by their example; and while he plumes himself upon the security of his title to the crown, should remember that, as it was acquired by one revolution, it may be lost by another.

JUNIUS.

LETTER XXXVI.

TO HIS GRACE THE DUKE OF GRAFTON.

MY LORD, 14. *Feb.* 1770.

IF I were personally your enemy, I might pity and forgive you. You have every claim to compassion, that can arise from misery and distress. The condition you are reduced to would disarm a private enemy of his resentment, and leave no consolation to the most vindictive spirit, but that such an object, as you are, would disgrace the dignity of revenge. But in the relation you have borne to this country, you have no title to indulgence; and if I had fol-

followed the dictates of my own opinion, I never ſhould have allowed you the reſpit of a moment. In your public character, you have injured every ſubject of the empire; and though an individual is not authoriſed to forgive the injuries done to ſociety, he is called upon to aſſert his ſeparate ſhare in the public reſentment. I ſubmitted however to the judgment of men, more moderate, perhaps more candid than myſelf. For my own part, I do not pretend to underſtand thoſe prudent forms of decorum, thoſe gentle rules of diſcretion, which ſome men endeavour to unite with the conduct of the greateſt and moſt hazardous affairs. Engaged in the defence of an honourable cauſe, I would take a deciſive part.—I ſhould ſcorn to provide for a future retreat, or to keep terms with a man, who preſerves no meaſures with the public. Neither the abject ſubmiſſion of deſerting his poſt in the hour of danger, nor even the * ſacred ſhield of cowardice ſhould protect him. I would purſue him through life, and try the laſt exertion of my abilities to preſerve the periſhable infamy of his name, and make it immortal.

* ——— *Sacro tremuere timore.* Every coward pretends to be planet-ſtruck.

WHAT

WHAT then, my Lord, is this the event of all the ſacrifices you have made to Lord Bute's patronage, and to your own unfortunate ambition? Was it for this you abandoned your earlieſt friendſhips,—the warmeſt connexions of your youth, and all thoſe honourable engagements, by which you once ſolicited, and might have acquired the eſteem of your country? Have you ſecured no recompence for ſuch a waſte of honour?—Unhappy man! what party will receive the common deſerter of all parties? Without a client to flatter, without a friend to conſole you, and with only one companion from the honeſt houſe of Bloomſbury, you muſt now retire into a dreadful ſolitude. At the moſt active period of life, you muſt quit the buſy ſcene, and conceal yourſelf from the world, if you would hope to ſave the wretched remains of a ruined reputation. The vices operate like age,—bring on diſeaſe before its time, and in the prime of youth leave the character broken and exhauſted.

YET your conduct has been myſterious, as well as contemptible. Where is now that firmneſs, or obſtinacy ſo long boaſted of by your

your friends, and acknowledged by your enemies? We were taught to expect, that you would not leave the ruin of this country to be compleated by other hands, but were determined either to gain a decisive victory over the constitution, or to perish bravely at least behind the last dike of the prerogative. You knew the danger, and might have been provided for it. You took sufficient time to prepare for a meeting with your parliament, to confirm the mercenary fidelity of your dependants, and to suggest to your Sovereign a language suited to his dignity at least, if not to his benevolence and wisdom. Yet, while the whole kingdom was agitated with anxious expectation upon one great point, you meanly evaded the question, and, instead of the explicit firmness and decision of a King, gave us nothing but the misery of a ruined * grazier, and the whining piety of a Methodist. We had reason to expect, that notice would have been taken of the petitions which the king has received from the English nation; and although I can conceive some personal motives for not yielding to them, I can find none, in common prudence

* There was something wonderfully pathetic in the mention of the horned cattle.

or decency, for treating them with contempt. Be aſſured, my Lord, the Engliſh people will not tamely ſubmit to this unworthy treatment;—they had a right to be heard, and their petitions, if not granted, deſerved to be conſidered. Whatever be the real views and doctrine of a court, the Sovereign ſhould be taught to preſerve ſome forms of attention to his ſubjects, and if he will not redreſs their grievances, not to make them a topic of jeſt and mockery among lords and ladies of the bedchamber. Injuries may be atoned for and forgiven; but inſults admit of no compenſation. They degrade the mind in its own eſteem, and force it to recover its level by revenge. This neglect of the petitions was however a part of your original plan of government, nor will any conſequences it has produced account for your deſerting your Sovereign, in the midſt of that diſtreſs, in which you and your * new friends had involved him. One would think, my Lord, you might have taken this ſpirited reſolution before you had diſſolved the laſt of thoſe early connexions, which once, even in your own opinion, did honour to your youth;—before you had obliged Lord Granby to quit

* The Bedford party.

a ſera ſervice he was attached to;—before you had diſcarded one chancellor, and killed another. To what an abject condition have you laboured to reduce the beſt of princes, when the unhappy man, who yields at laſt to ſuch perſonal inſtance and ſolicitation, as never can be fairly employed againſt a ſubject, feels himſelf degraded by his compliance, and is unable to ſurvive the diſgraceful honours which his gracious Sovereign had compelled him to accept. He was a man of ſpirit, for he had a quick ſenſe of ſhame, and death has redeemed his character. I know your Grace too well to appeal to your feelings upon this event; but there is another heart, not yet, I hope, quite callous to the touch of humanity, to which it ought to be a dreadful leſſon for ever *.

Now, my Lord, let us conſider the ſituation to which you have conducted, and in which you have thought it adviſeable to abandon your royal maſter. Whenever the people have complained, and nothing better could be ſaid in defence of the meaſures of govern-

* The moſt ſecret particulars of this deteſtable tranſaction ſhall, in due time, be given to the public. The people ſhall know what kind of man they have to deal with.

ment,

ment, it has been the faſhion to anſwer us, though not very fairly, with an appeal to the private virtues of your Sovereign. "Has he "not, to relieve the people, ſurrendered a "conſiderable part of his revenue?—Has he "not made the judges independent, by fix-"ing them in their places for life?"—My Lord, we acknowledge the gracious principle, which gave birth to theſe conceſſions, and have nothing to regret, but that it has never been adhered to. At the end of ſeven years, we are loaded with a debt of above five hundred thouſand pounds upon the civil liſt, and we now ſee the Chancellor of Great Britain tyrannically forced out of his office, not for want of abilities, not for want of integrity, or of attention to his duty, but for delivering his honeſt opinion in parliament, upon the greateſt conſtitutional queſtion, that has ariſen ſince the revolution.—We care not to whoſe private virtues you appeal; the theory of ſuch a government is falſehood and mockery;—the practice is oppreſſion. You have laboured then (though I confeſs to no purpoſe) to rob your maſter of the only plauſible anſwer, that ever was given in defence of his government,—of the opinion, which the people had conceived of his perſonal ho-

nour

nour and integrity.—The Duke of Bedford was more moderate than your Grace. He only forced his maſter to violate a ſolemn promiſe made to an * individual. But you, my Lord, have ſucceſsfully extended your advice to every political, every moral engagement, that could bind either the magiſtrate or the man. The condition of a King is often miſerable, but it required your Grace's abilities to make it contemptible.—You will ſay perhaps that the faithful ſervants, in whoſe hands you have left him, are able to retrieve his honour, and to ſupport his government. You have publicly declared, even ſince your reſignation, that you approved of their meaſures, and admired their conduct,—particularly that of the Earl of Sandwich. What a pity it is, that, with all this appearance, you ſhould think it neceſſary to ſeparate yourſelf from ſuch amiable companions. You forget, my Lord, that while you are laviſh in the praiſe of men whom you deſert, you are publicly oppoſing your conduct to your opinions, and depriving yourſelf of the only plauſible pretence you had for leaving your Sovereign overwhelmed with diſtreſs; I call it plauſible,

* Mr. Stuart Mackenzie.

for,

for, in truth, there is no reaſon whatſoever, leſs than the frowns of your maſter, that could juſtify a man of ſpirit for abandoning his poſt at a moment ſo critical and important? It is in vain to evade the queſtion. If you will not ſpeak out, the public have a right to judge from appearances. We are authorized to conclude, that you either differed from your colleagues, whoſe meaſures you ſtill affect to defend, or that you thought the adminiſtration of the King's affairs no longer tenable. You are at liberty to chooſe between the hypocrite and the coward. Your beſt friends are in doubt which way they ſhall incline. Your country unites the characters, and gives you credit for them both. For my own part, I ſee nothing inconſiſtent in your conduct. You began with betraying the people,——you conclude with betraying the King.

In your treatment of particular perſons, you have preſerved the uniformity of your character. Even Mr. Bradſhaw declares, that no man was ever ſo ill uſed as himſelf. As to the proviſion * you have made for his family,

* A penſion of 1500 *l.* per annum, inſured upon the 4 1-half per cents, (he was too cunning to truſt to Iriſh ſecurity) for the

family, he was intitled to it by the houſe he lives in. The ſucceſſor of one Chancellor might well pretend to be the rival of another. It is the breach of private friendſhip which touches Mr. Bradſhaw; and to ſay the truth, when a man of his rank and abilities had taken ſo active a part in your affairs, he ought not to have been let down at laſt with a miſerable penſion of fifteen hundred pounds a year. Colonel Luttrell, Mr. Onſlow, and Governor Burgoyne, were equally engaged with you, and have rather more reaſon to complain than Mr. Bradſhaw. Theſe are men, my Lord, whoſe friendſhip you ſhould have adhered to on the ſame principle, on which you deſerted Lord Rockingham, Lord

the lives of himſelf and all his ſons. This gentleman, who a very few years ago was clerk to a contractor for forage, and afterwards exalted to a petty poſt in the war office, thought it neceſſary (as ſoon as he was appointed Secretary to the Treaſury) to take that great houſe in Lincoln's-Inn-Fields, in which the Earl of Northington had reſided, while he was Lord High Chancellor of Great Britain. As to the penſion, Lord North very ſolemnly aſſured the houſe of commons, that no penſion was ever ſo well deſerved as Mr. Bradſhaw's---- N. B. Lord Camden and Sir Jeffery Amherſt are not near ſo well provided for, and Sir Edward Hawke, who ſaved the ſtate, retires with two thouſand pounds a year, on the Iriſh eſtabliſhment, from which he in fact receives leſs than Mr. Bradſhaw's penſion.

 Chatham,

Chatham, Lord Camden, and the Duke of Portland. We can easily account for your violating your engagements with men of honour, but why should you betray your natural connexions? Why separate yourself from Lord Sandwich, Lord Gower, and Mr. Rigby, or leave the three worthy gentlemen abovementioned to shift for themselves? With all the fashionable indulgence of the times, this country does not abound in characters like theirs; and you may find it a difficult matter to recruit the black catalogue of your friends.

THE recollection of the royal patent you sold to Mr. Hine, obliges me to say a word in defence of a man whom you have taken the most dishonourable means to injure. I do not refer to the sham prosecution which you affected to carry on against him. On that ground, I doubt not he is prepared to meet you with tenfold recrimination, and set you at defiance. The injury you had done him affects his moral character. You knew that the offer to purchase the reversion of a place, which has heretofore been sold under a decree of the court of Chancery, however imprudent in his situation, would no way tend to cover him with that ſort of guilt which you wiſhed to fix upon him in the eyes of the world. You laboured then, by every ſpecies of falſe ſuggeſtion, and even by publiſhing counterfeit letters, to have it underſtood that he had propoſed terms of accommodation to you, and had offered to abandon his principles, his party, and his friends. You conſulted your own breaſt for a character of conſummate treachery, and gave it to the public for that of Mr. Vaughan. I think myſelf obliged to do this juſtice to an injured man, becauſe I was deceived by the appearances thrown out by your Grace, and have frequently ſpoken of his conduct with indignation. If he really be, what I think him, honeſt, though miſtaken, he will be happy in recovering his reputation, though at the expence of his underſtanding. Here, I ſee, the matter is likely to reſt. Your Grace is afraid to carry on the proſecution. Mr. Hine keeps quiet poſſeſſion of his purchaſe; and Governor Burgoyne, relieved from the apprehenſion of refunding the money, ſits down, for the remainder of his life, INFAMOUS AND CONTENTED.

I BELIEVE, my Lord, I may now take my leave of you for ever. You are no longer that refolute minifter, who had fpirit to fupport the moft violent meafures; who compenfated for the want of good and great qualities, by a brave determination, (which fome people admired and relied on) to maintain himfelf without them. The reputation of obftinacy and perfeverance might have fupplied the place of all the abfent virtues. You have now added the laft negative to your character, and meanly confeffed that you are deftitute of the common fpirit of a man. Retire then, my Lord, and hide your blufhes from the world; for, with fuch a load of fhame, even BLACK may change its colour. A mind fuch as yours, in the folitary hours of domeftic enjoyment, may ftill find topics of confolation. You may find it in the memory of violated friendfhip; in the afflictions of an accomplifhed prince, whom you have difgraced and deferted, and in the agitations of a great country, driven, by your councils, to the brink of deftruction.

THE palm of minifterial firmnefs is now transferred to Lord North. He tells us fo him-

himſelf, with the plenitude of the *ore rotundo* *; and I am ready enough to believe, that, while he can keep his place, he will not eaſily be perſuaded to reſign it. Your Grace was the firm miniſter of yeſterday: Lord North is the firm miniſter of to-day. To-morrow, perhaps, his Majeſty, in his wiſdom, may give us a rival for you both. You are too well acquainted with the temper of your late allies, to think it poſſible that Lord North ſhould be permitted to govern this country. If we may believe common fame, they have ſhewn him their ſuperiority already. His Majeſty is indeed too gracious to inſult his ſubjects, by chuſing his firſt miniſter from among the domeſtics of the Duke of Bedford. That would have been too groſs an outrage to the three kingdoms. Their purpoſe, however, is equally anſwered by puſhing forward this unhappy figure, and forcing it to bear the odium of meaſures, which they in reality direct. Without immediately appearing to govern, they poſſeſs the power, and diſtribute the emoluments of government as they think proper. They

* This eloquent perſon has got as far as the *diſcipline* of Demoſthenes. He conſtantly ſpeaks with pebbles in his mouth, to improve his articulation.

ſtill adhere to the ſpirit of that calculation, which made Mr. Luttrell repreſentative of Middleſex. Far from regretting your retreat, they aſſure us very gravely, that it increaſes the real ſtrength of the miniſtry. According to this way of reaſoning, they will probably grow ſtronger, and more flouriſhing, every hour they exiſt; for I think there is hardly a day paſſes in which ſome one or other of his Majeſty's ſervants does not leave them to improve by the loſs of his aſſiſtance. But, alas! their countenances ſpeak a different language. When the members drop off, the main body cannot be inſenſible of its approaching diſſolution. Even the violence of their proceedings is a ſignal of deſpair. Like broken tenants, who have had warning to quit the premiſes, they curſe their landlord, deſtroy the fixtures, throw every thing into confuſion, and care not what miſchief they do to the eſtate.

JUNIUS.

LETTER XXXVII.

TO THE PRINTER OF THE PUBLIC ADVERTISER.

SIR, 19. *March*, 1770.

I Believe there is no man, however indifferent about the interests of this country, who will not readily confess that the situation, to which we are now reduced, whether it has arisen from the violence of faction, or from an arbitrary system of government, justifies the most melancholy apprehensions, and calls for the exertion of whatever wisdom or vigour is left among us. The King's answer to the remonstrance of the city of London, and the measures since adopted by the ministry, amount to a plain declaration, that the principle, on which Mr. Luttrell was seated in the house of commons, is to be supported in all its consequences, and carried to its utmost extent. The same spirit, which violated the freedom of election, now invades the declaration and bill of rights, and threatens to punish the subject for exercising a privilege, hitherto undisputed, of petitioning the crown. The grievances of the people are aggravated by insults; their complaints not merely disregarded, but checked by authority; and every one of those acts, against which they remonstrated, confirmed by the King's decisive approbation. At such a moment, no honest man will remain silent or inactive. However distinguished by rank or property, in the rights of freedom we are all equal. As we are Englishmen, the least considerable man among us has an interest equal to the proudest nobleman, in the laws and constitution of his country, and is equally called upon to make a generous contribution in support of them;—whether it be the heart to conceive, the understanding to direct, or the hand to execute. It is a common cause, in which we are all interested, in which we should all be engaged. The man who deserts it at this alarming crisis, is an enemy to his country, and, what I think of infinitely less importance, a traitor to his Sovereign. The subject, who is truly loyal to the chief magistrate, will neither advise nor submit to arbitrary measures. The city of London have given an example, which, I doubt not, will be followed by the whole kingdom. The

noble

noble ſpirit of the metropolis is the life-blood of the ſtate, collected at the heart: from that point it circulates, with health and vigour, through every artery of the conſtitution. The time is come, when the body of the Engliſh people muſt aſſert their own cauſe: conſcious of their ſtrength, and animated by a ſenſe of their duty, they will not ſurrender their birthright to miniſters, parliaments, or kings.

THE city of London have expreſſed their ſentiments with freedom and firmneſs; they have ſpoken truth boldly; and, in whatever light their remonſtrance may be repreſented by courtiers, I defy the moſt ſubtle lawyer in this country to point out a ſingle inſtance, in which they have exceeded the truth. Even that aſſertion, which we are told is moſt offenſive to parliament, in the theory of the Engliſh conſtitution, is ſtrictly true. If any part of the repreſentative body be not choſen by the people, that part vitiates and corrupts the whole. If there be a defect in the repreſentation of the people, that power, which alone is equal to the making of the laws in this country, is not complete, and the acts of parliament under that circumſtance, are not the acts of a pure and entire legiflature. I fpeak of the theory of our conftitution; and whatever difficulties or inconveniencies may attend the practice, I am ready to maintain, that, as far as the fact deviates from the principle, fo far the practice is vicious and corrupt. I have not heard a queftion raifed upon any other part of the remonftrance. That the principle, on which the Middlefex election was determined, is more pernicious in its effects, than either the levying of fhip-money, by Charles the Firft, or the fufpending power affumed by his fon, will hardly be difputed by any man who underftands or wifhes well to the Englifh conftitution. It is not an act of open violence done by the King, or any direct or palpable breach of the laws attempted by his minifter, that can ever endanger the liberties of this country. Againft fuch a King or minifter the people would immediately take the alarm, and all the parties unite to oppofe him. The laws may be grofsly violated in particular inftances, without any direct attack upon the whole fyftem. Facts of that kind ftand alone; they are attributed to neceffity, not defended by principle. We can never be really in danger, until the forms of parliament are made ufe of to

deftroy

destroy the substance of our civil and political liberties;—until parliament itself betrays its trust, by contributing to establish new principles of government, and employing the very weapons committed to it by the collective body, to stab the constitution.

As for the terms of the remonstrance, I presume it will not be affirmed, by any person less polished than a gentleman usher, that this is a season for compliments. Our gracious King indeed is abundantly civil to himself. Instead of an answer to a petition, his majesty, very gracefully pronounces his own panegyric; and I confess, that, as far as his personal behaviour, or the royal purity of his intentions is concerned, the truth of those declarations, which the minister has drawn up for his master, cannot decently be disputed. In every other respect, I affirm, that they are absolutely unsupported, either in argument or fact. I must add too, that supposing the speech were otherwise unexceptionable, it is not a direct answer to the petition of the city. His Majesty is pleased to say, that he is always ready to receive the requests of his subjects; yet the sheriffs were twice sent back with an excuse, and it was

certainly

certainly debated in council whether or no the magiſtrates of the city of London ſhould be admitted to an audience. Whether the remonſtrance be or be not injurious to parliament,is the very queſtion between the parliament and the people, and ſuch a queſtion as cannot be decided by the aſſertion of a third party, however reſpectable. That the petitioning for a diſſolution of parliament is irreconcileable with the principles of the conſtitution is a new doctrine. His Majeſty perhaps has not been informed, that the houſe of commons themſelves have, by a formal reſolution, admitted it to be the right of the ſubject. His Majeſty proceeds to aſſure us that he has made the laws the rule of his conduct.—Was it in ordering or permitting his miniſters to apprehend Mr. Wilkes by a general warrant?—Was is in ſuffering his miniſters to revive the obſolete maxim of *nullum tempus* to rob the Duke of Portland of his property, and thereby give a deciſive turn to a county election?—Was it in erecting a chamber conſultation of ſurgeons, with authority to examine into and ſuperſede the legal verdict of a jury? Or did his Majeſty conſult the laws of this country, when he

per-

permitted his secretary of state to declare, that whenever the civil magistrate is trifled with, a military force must be sent for, *without the delay of a moment*, and effectually employed? Or was it in the barbarous exactness with which this illegal, inhuman doctrine was carried into execution?—If his Majesty had recollected these facts, I think he would never have said, at least with any reference to the measures of his government, that he had made the laws the rule of his conduct. To talk of preserving the affections, or relying on the support of his subjects, while he continues to act upon these principles, is indeed paying a compliment to their loyalty, which I hope they have too much spirit and understanding to deserve.

HIS Majesty, we are told, is not only punctual in the performance of his own duty, but careful not to assume any of those powers which the constitution has placed in other hands. Admitting this last assertion to be strictly true, it is no way to the purpose. The city of London have not desired the King to assume a power placed in other hands. If they had, I should hope to see the person, who dared to present such a petition, immediately impeached. They solicit

cit their Sovereign to exert that constitutional authority, which the laws have vested in him, for the benefit of his subjects. They call upon him to make use of his lawful prerogative in a case, which our laws evidently supposed might happen, since they have provided for it by trusting the Sovereign with a discretionary power to dissolve the parliament. This request will, I am confident, be supported by remonstrances from all parts of the kingdom. His Majesty will find at last, that this is the sense of his people, and that it is not his interest to support either ministry or parliament, at the hazard of a breach with the collective body of his subjects.—That he is the King of a free people, is indeed his greatest glory. That he may long continue the King of a free people, is the second wish that animates my heart. The first is, THAT THE PEOPLE MAY BE FREE.*

JUNIUS.

* When his Majesty had done reading his speech, the Lord Mayor, &c. had the honour of kissing his Majesty's hand; after which, as they were withdrawing, his Majesty instantly turned round to his courtiers, *and burst out a laughimg.*

Nero fiddled, while Rome was burning. JOHN HORNE.

LET-

LETTER XXXVIII.

TO THE PRINTER OF THE PUBLIC ADVERTISER.

SIR, 3. *April*, 1770.

IN my laſt letter I offered you my opinion of the truth and propriety of his Majeſty's anſwer to the city of London, conſidering it merely as the ſpeech of a miniſter, drawn up in his own defence, and delivered, as uſual, by the chief magiſtrate. I would ſeparate, as much as poſſible, the King's perſonal character and behaviour from the acts of the preſent government. I wiſh it to be underſtood that his Majeſty had in effect no more concern in the ſubſtance of what he ſaid, than Sir James Hodges had in the remonſtrance, and that as Sir James, in virtue of his office, was obliged to ſpeak the ſentiments of the people, his Majeſty might think himſelf bound, by the ſame official obligation, to give a graceful utterance to the ſentiments of his miniſter. The cold formality of of a well repeated leſſon is widely diſtant from the animated expreſſion of the heart.

THIS diſtinction, however, is only true with reſpect to the meaſure itſelf. The conſequences of it reach beyond the miniſter, and materially affect his Majeſty's honour. In their own nature they are formidable enough to alarm a man of prudence, and diſgraceful enough to afflict a man of ſpirit. A ſubject, whoſe ſincere attachment to his Majeſty's perſon and family is founded upon rational principles, will not, in the preſent conjuncture, be ſcrupulous of alarming, or even of afflicting his Sovereign. I know there is another ſort of loyalty, of which his Majeſty has had plentiful experience. When the loyalty of Tories, Jacobites, and Scotchmen, has once taken poſſeſſion of an unhappy Prince, it ſeldom leaves him without accompliſhing his deſtruction. When the poiſon of their doctrines has tainted the natural benevolence of his diſpoſition, when their inſidious counſels have corrupted the *ſtamina* of his government, what antidote can reſtore him to his political health and honour, but the firm ſincerity of his Engliſh ſubjects?

It has not been uſual in this country, at leaſt ſince the days of Charles the firſt, to ſee the ſovereign perſonally at variance, or engaged in a direct altercation with his ſubjects. Acts of grace and indulgence are wiſely appropriated to him, and ſhould conſtantly be performed by himſelf. He never ſhould appear but in an amiable light to his ſubjects. Even in France, as long as any ideas of a limited monarchy were thought worth preſerving, it was a maxim, that no man ſhould leave the royal preſence diſcontented. They have loſt or renounced the moderate principles of their government, and now, when their parliaments venture to remonſtrate, the tyrant comes forward, and anſwers abſolntely for himſelf. The ſpirit of their preſent conſtitution requires that the King ſhould be feared, and the principle, I believe, is tolerably ſupported by the fact. But, in our political ſyſtem, the theory is at variance with the practice, for the King ſhould be beloved. Meaſures of greater ſeverity may, indeed, in ſome circumſtances, be neceſſary; but the miniſter who adviſes, ſhould take the execution and odium of them entirely upon himſelf. He not only betrays his maſter, but violates the ſpirit of the Engliſh conſtitution, when he expoſes the chief magiſtrate to the perſonal hatred or contempt of his ſubjects. When we ſpeak of the firmneſs of government, we, mean an uniform ſyſtem of meaſures, deliberately adopted, and reſolutely maintained by the ſervants of the crown, not a peeviſh aſperity in the language or behaviour of the ſovereign. The government of a weak, irreſolute monarch may be wiſe, moderate, and firm;—that of an obſtinate capricious prince, on the contrary, may be feeble, undetermined and relaxed. The reputation of public meaſures depends upon the miniſter, who is reſponſible, not upon the King, whoſe private opinions are not ſuppoſed to have any weight againſt the advice of his counſel, whoſe perſonal authority ſhould therefore never be interpoſed in public affairs.—This, I believe, is true, conſtitutional doctrine. But for a moment let us ſuppoſe it falſe. Let it be taken for granted, that an occaſion may ariſe, in which a King of England ſhall be compelled to take upon himſelf the ungrateful office of rejecting the petitions, and cenſuring the conduct of his ſubjects; and let the City remonſtrance be ſuppoſed to have created ſo extraordinary an occaſion. On this principle, which I preſume no friend of adminiſtration will diſpute, let the wiſdom

and

and ſpirit of the miniſtry be examined. They adviſe the King to hazard his dignity, by a poſitive declaration of his own ſentiments? —they ſuggeſt to him a language full of ſeverity and reproach. What follows? When his Majeſty had taken ſo deciſive a part in ſupport of his miniſtry and parliament, he had a right to expect from them a reciprocal demonſtration of firmneſs in their own cauſe, and of their zeal for his honour. He had reaſon to expect (and ſuch, I doubt not, were the bluſtering promiſes of Lord North) that the perſons, whom he had been adviſed to charge with having failed in their reſpect to him, with having injured parliament, and violated the principles of the conſtitution, ſhould not have been permitted to eſcape without ſome ſevere marks of the diſpleaſure and vengeance of parliament. As the matter ſtands, the miniſter, after placing his ſovereign in the moſt unfavourable light to his ſubjects, and after attempting to fix the ridicule and odium of his own precipitate meaſures upon the royal character, leaves him a ſolitary figure upon the ſcene, to recal, if he can, or to compenſate, by future compliances, for one unhappy demonſtration of ill-ſupported firmneſs, and ineffectual re-

 ſentment.

ſentment. As a man of ſpirit, his Majeſty cannot but be ſenſible, that the lofty terms in which he was perſuaded to reprimand the city, when united with the ſilly concluſion of the buſineſs, reſemble the pomp of a mock-tragedy, where the moſt pathetic ſentiments, and even the ſufferings of the hero are calculated for deriſion.

SUCH has been the boaſted firmneſs and conſiſtency of a miniſter, * whoſe appearance in the houſe of commons was thought eſſential to the King's ſervice;—whoſe preſence was to influence every diviſion;—who had a voice to perſuade, an eye to penetrate, a geſture to command. The reputation of theſe great qualities has been fatal to his friends. The little dignity of Mr. Ellis has been committed. The mine was ſunk;—combuſtibles provided, and Welbore Ellis, the Guy Faux of the fable, waited only for the ſignal of command. All of a ſudden the country gentlemen diſcover how groſsly

* This graceful miniſter is oddly conſtructed. His tongue is a little too big for his mouth, and his eyes a great deal too big for their ſockets. Every part of his perſon ſets natural proportion at defiance. At this preſent writing, his head is ſuppoſed to be much too heavy for his ſhoulders.

they

they have been deceived;—the miniſter's heart fails him, the grand plot is defeated in a moment, and poor Mr. Ellis and his motion taken into cuſtody. From the event of Friday laſt, one would imagine, that ſome fatality hung over this gentleman. Whether he makes or ſuppreſſes a motion, he is equally ſure of his diſgrace. But the complexion of the times will ſuffer no man to be vice-treaſurer of Ireland with impunity *.

I do not mean to expreſs the ſmalleſt anxiety for the miniſter's reputation. He acts ſeparately for himſelf, and the moſt ſhameful inconſiſtency may perhaps be no

* About this time, the courtiers talked of nothing but a bill of pains and penalties againſt the Lord Mayor and Sheriffs, or impeachment at the leaſt. Little *Mannikin Ellis* told the King that, if the buſineſs were left to his management, he would engage to do wonders. It was thought very odd that a motion of ſo much importance ſhould be intruſted to the moſt contemptible little piece of machinery in the whole kingdom. His honeſt zeal however was diſappointed. The miniſter took fright, and at the very inſtant that little Ellis was going to open, ſent him an order to ſit down. All their magnanimous threats ended in a ridiculous vote of cenſure, and a ſtill more ridiculous addreſs to the King. This ſhameful deſertion ſo afflicted the generous mind of George the Third, that he was obliged to live upon potatoes for three weeks, to keep off a malignant fever.---Poor man!---*quis talia fando temperet a lacrymis!*

disgrace to him. But when the Sovereign, who represents the majesty of the state, appears in person, his dignity should be supported. The occasion should be important;—the plan well considered;—the execution steady and consistent. My zeal for his Majesty's real honour compels me to assert, that it has been too much the system of the present reign, to introduce him personally, either to act for, or to defend his servants. They persuade him to do what is properly *their* business, and desert him in the midst of it*. Yet this is an inconvenience, to which he must for ever be exposed, while he adheres to a ministry divided among themselves, or unequal in credit and ability to the great task they have undertaken. Instead of reserving the interposition of the royal personage, as the last resource of government, their weakness obliges them to apply it to every ordinary occasion, and to render it cheap and common in the opinion of the people. Instead of supporting their master, they look to

* After a certain person had succeeded in cajolling Mr. Yorke, he told the Duke of Grafton, with a witty smile, "My Lord, you may kill the next Percy yourself."--- N. B. He had but that instant wiped the tears away, which overcame Mr. Yorke.

him

him for ſupport; and, for the emoluments of remaining one day more in office, care not how much his ſacred character is proſtituted and diſhonoured.

IF I thought it poſſible for this paper to reach the cloſet, I would venture to appeal at once to his Majeſty's judgement. I would aſk him, but in the moſt reſpectful terms, "As you are a young man, Sir, who ought "to have a life of happineſs in proſpect;— "as you are a huſband;—as you are a father, "[your filial duties I own have been reli-"giouſly performed] is it *bona fide* for your "intereſt or your honor to ſacrifice your do-"meſtic tranquillity, and to live in a per-"petual diſagreement with your people, "merely to preſerve ſuch a chain of beings "as North, Barrington, Weymouth, Gower, "Ellis, Onſlow, Rigby, Jerry Dyſon, and "Sandwich? Their very names are a ſatire "upon all government, and I defy the graveſt "of your chaplains to read the catalogue "without laughing."

FOR my own part, Sir, I have always conſidered addreſſes from parliament as a faſhionable, unmeaning formality. Uſurpers, ideots, and tyrants have been ſucceſſively complimented with almoſt the ſame profeſſions of duty and affection. But let us ſuppoſe them to mean exactly what they profeſs. The conſequences deſerve to be conſidered. Either the ſovereign is a man of high ſpirit and dangerous ambition, ready to take advantage of the treachery of his parliament, ready to accept of the ſurrender they make him of the public liberty;—or he is a mild, undeſigning prince, who, provided they indulge him with a little ſtate and pageantry, would of himſelf intend no miſchief. On the firſt ſuppoſition, it muſt ſoon be decided by the ſword, whether the conſtitution ſhould be loſt or preſerved. On the ſecond, a prince no way qualified for the execution of a great and hazardous enterprize, and without any determined object in view, may nevertheleſs be driven into ſuch deſperate meaſures, as may lead directly to his ruin, or diſgrace himſelf by a ſhameful fluctuation between the extremes of violence at one moment, and timidity at another. The miniſter perhaps may have reaſon to be ſatisfied with the ſucceſs of the preſent hour, and with the profits of his employment. He is the tenant of the day, and has no intereſt in the inheritance. The ſovereign himſelf is bound

bound by other obligations, and ought to look forward to a ſuperior, a permanent intereſt. His paternal tenderneſs ſhould remind him, how many hoſtages he has given to ſociety. The ties of nature come powerfully in aid of oaths and proteſtations. The father, who conſiders his own precarious ſtate of health, and the poſſible hazard of a long minority, will wiſh to ſee the family eſtate free and unincumbered.*. What is the dignity of the crown, though it were really maintained;—what is the honour of parliament, ſuppoſing it could exiſt without any foundation of integrity and juſtice;—or what is the vain reputation of firmneſs, even if the ſcheme of the government were uniform and conſiſtent, compared with the heart-felt affections of the people, with the happineſs and ſecurity of the royal family, or even with the grateful acclamations of the populace! Whatever ſtyle of contempt may be adopted by miniſters or parliaments, no man ſincerely deſpiſes the voice of the Engliſh nation. The houſe of commons are only interpreters, whoſe duty it is

* Every true friend of the Houſe of Brunſwick ſees with affliction, how rapidly ſome of the principal branches of the family have dropped off.

to convey the ſenſe of the people faithfully to the crown. If the interpretation be falſe or imperfect, the conſtituent powers are called upon to deliver their own ſentiments. Their ſpeech is rude, but intelligible;—their geſtures fierce, but full of explanation. Perplexed by ſophiſtries, their honeſt eloquence riſes into action. Their firſt appeal was to the integrity of their repreſentatives:—the ſecond to the King's juſtice;—the laſt argument of the people, whenever they have recourſe to it, will carry more perhaps than perſuaſion to parliament, or ſupplication to the throne.

JUNIUS.

LETTER XXXIX.

TO THE PRINTER OF THE PUBLIC ADVERTISER.

SIR, 28. *May* 1770.

WHILE parliament was ſitting, it would neither have been ſafe, nor perhaps quite regular, to offer any opinion to the public, upon the juſtice or wiſdom of their proceedings. To pronounce fairly upon their conduct, it was neceſſary to wait until we could conſider, in one view, the beginning, progreſs, and concluſion of their deliberations. The cauſe of the public was undertaken and ſupported by men, whoſe abilities and united authority, to ſay nothing of the advantageous ground they ſtood on, might well be thought ſufficient to determine a popular queſtion in favour of the people. Neither was the houſe of commons ſo abſolutely engaged in defence of the miniſtry, or even of their own reſolutions, but that *they* might have paid ſome decent regard to the known diſpoſition of their conſtituents, and, without any diſhonour to their firmneſs, might have retracted an opinion too haſtily adopted, when they ſaw the alarm it had created, and how ſtrongly it was oppoſed by the general ſenſe of the nation. The miniſtry too would have conſulted their own immediate intereſt, in making ſome conceſſion ſatisfactory to the moderate part of the people. Without touching the fact, they might have conſented to guard againſt, or give up the dangerous principle, on which it was eſtabliſhed. In this ſtate of things, I think it was highly improbable at the beginning of the ſeſſion, that the complaints of the people upon a matter, which, in *their* apprehenſion at leaſt, immediately

diately affected the life of the conſtitution, would be treated with as much contempt by their own repreſentatives, and by the houſe of lords, as they had been by the other branch of the legiſlature. Deſpairing of their integrity, we had a right to expect ſomething from their prudence, and ſomething from their fears. The Duke of Grafton certainly did not foreſee to what an extent the corruption of a parliament might be carried. He thought, perhaps, that there was ſtill ſome portion of ſhame or virtue left in the majority of the houſe of commons, or that there was a line in public proſtitution, beyond which they would ſcruple to proceed. Had the young man been a little more practiſed in the world, or had he ventured to meaſure the characters of other men by his own, he would not have been ſo eaſily diſcouraged.

The prorogation of parliament naturally calls upon us to review their proceedings, and to conſider the condition in which they have left the kingdom. I do not queſtion but they have done what is uſually called the King's buſineſs, much to his Majeſty's ſatisfaction. We have only to lament, that, in conſequence of a ſyſtem introduced or revived

vived in the present reign, this kind of merit should be very consistent with the neglect of every duty they owe to the nation. The interval between the opening of the last and close of the former session was longer than usual. Whatever were the views of the minister in deferring the meeting of parliament, sufficient time was certainly given to every member of the house of commons, to look back upon the steps he had taken, and the consequences they had produced. The zeal of party, the violence of personal animosities, and the heat of contention had leisure to subside. From that period, whatever resolution they took was deliberate and prepense. In the preceding session, the dependents of the ministry had affected to believe, that the final determination of the question would have satisfied the nation, or at least put a stop to their complaints; as if the certainty of an evil could diminish the sense of it, or the nature of injustice could be altered by decision. But they found the people of England were in a temper very distant from submission; and, although it was contended that the house of commons could not themselves reverse a resolution, which had the force and effect of a judicial sentence, there were other constitu-

tional

tional expedients, which would have given a ſecurity againſt any ſimilar attempts for the future. The general propoſition, in which the whole country had an intereſt, might have been reduced to a particular fact, in which Mr. Wilkes and Mr. Luttrell would alone have been concerned. The houſe of lords might interpoſe ;—the King might diſſolve the parliament ;—or, if every other reſource failed, there ſtill lay a grand conſtitutional writ of error, in behalf of the people, from the deciſion of one court to the wiſdom of the whole legiſlature. Every one of theſe remedies has been ſucceſſively attempted. The people performed *their* part with dignity, ſpirit, and perſeverance. For many months his Majeſty heard nothing from his people but the language of complaint and reſentment ;—unhappily for this country, it was the daily triumph of his courtiers that he heard it with an indifference approaching to contempt.

THE houſe of commons having aſſumed a power unknown to the conſtitution, were determined not merely to ſupport it in the ſingle inſtance in queſtion, but to maintain the doctrine in its utmoſt extent, and to eſtab-

eſtabliſh the fact as a precedent in law, to be applied in whatever manner his Majeſty's ſervants ſhould hereafter think fit. Their proceedings upon this occaſion are a ſtrong proof that a deciſion, in the firſt inſtance illegal and unjuſt, can only be ſupported by a continuation of falſehood and injuſtice. To ſupport their former reſolutions, they were obliged to violate ſome of the beſt known and eſtabliſhed rules of the houſe. In one inſtance they went ſo far as to declare, in open defiance of truth and common ſenſe, that it was not the rule of the houſe to divide a complicated queſtion, at the requeſt of a member *. But after trampling upon the laws of the land, it was not wonderful that they ſhould treat the private regulations of their own aſſembly with equal diſregard. The ſpeaker, being young in office, began with pretended ignorance, and ended with deciding for the miniſtry. We were not ſurprized at the deciſion; but he heſitated

* This extravagant reſolution appears in the Votes of the houſe; but, in the minutes of the committees, the inſtances of reſolutions contrary to law and truth, or of refuſals to acknowledge law and truth when propoſed to them, are innumerable.

and

and blushed at his own baseness, and every man was astonished *.

THE interest of the public was vigorously supported in the house of lords. Their right to defend the constitution against an incroachment of the other estates, and the necessity of exerting it at this period, was urged to them with every argument, that could be supposed to influence the heart or the understanding. But it soon appeared, that they had already taken their part, and were determined to support the house of commons, not only at the expence of truth and decency, but even by a surrender of their own most important rights. Instead of performing that

* When the King first made it a measure of his government to destroy Mr. Wilkes, and when for this purpose it was necessary to run down privilege, Sir Fletcher Norton, with his usual prostituted effrontery, assured the house of commons, that he should regard one of their votes, no more than a resolution of so many drunken porters. This is the very Lawyer, whom Ben Jonson describes in the following lines:

"Gives forked counsel; takes provoking gold,
"*On either hand*, and puts it up.
"So wise, so grave, of so perplex'd a tongue,
"And *loud* withal, that would not wag, nor scarce
"Lie still without *a fee*."

duty

duty which the conſtitution expected from them, in return for the dignity and independence of their ſtation, in return for the hereditary ſhare it has given them in the legiſlature, the majority of them made common cauſe with the other houſe in oppreſſing the people, and eſtabliſhed another doctrine as falſe in itſelf, and if poſſible more pernicious to the conſtitution, than that on which the Middleſex election was determined. By reſolving, "that they had no right to impeach "a judgment of the houſe of commons in "any caſe whatſoever, where that houſe has "a competent juriſdiction," they in effect gave up that conſtitutional check and reciprocal controul of one branch of the legiſlature over the other, which is perhaps the greateſt and moſt important object provided for by the diviſion of the whole legiſlative power into three eſtates; and now, let the judicial deciſions of the houſe of commons be ever ſo extravagant, let their declarations of the law be ever ſo flagrantly falſe, arbitrary, and oppreſſive to the ſubject, the houſe of lords have impoſed a ſlaviſh ſilence upon themſelves;—they cannot interpoſe,—they cannot protect the ſubject,—they cannot defend the laws of their country. A conceſſion ſo extraordinary in itſelf, ſo contradictory to the principles of their own inſtitution, cannot but alarm the moſt unſuſpecting mind. We may well conclude, that the lords would hardly have yielded ſo much to the other houſe, without the certainty of a compenſation, which can only be made to them at the expence of the people *. The arbitrary power they have aſſumed of impoſing fines and committing, during pleaſure, will now be exerciſed in its full extent. The houſe of commons are too much in their debt to queſtion or interrupt their proceedings. The crown too, we may be well aſſured, will loſe nothing in this new diſtribution of power. After declaring, that to petition for a diſſolution of parliament is irreconcileable with the principles of the conſtitution, his Majeſty has reaſon to expect that ſome extraordinary compliment will be returned to the Royal prerogative. The three branches of the legiſlature ſeem to treat their ſeparate rights and intereſts as the Roman Triumvirs

* The man who reſiſts and overcomes this iniquitous power, aſſumed by the lords, muſt be ſupported by the whole people. We have the laws of our ſide, and want nothing but an intrepid leader. When ſuch a man ſtands forth, let the nation look to it. It is not *his* cauſe, but our own.

did

did their friends. They reciprocally sacrifice them to the animosities of each other, and establish a detestable union among themselves, upon the ruin of the laws and liberty of the commonwealth.

THROUGH the whole proceedings of the house of commons in this session, there is an apparent, a palpable consciousness of guilt, which has prevented their daring to assert their own dignity, where it has been immediately and grossly attacked. In the course of Doctor Musgrave's examination, he said every thing that can be conceived mortifying to individuals, or offensive to the house. They voted his information frivolous, but they were awed by his firmness and integrity, and sunk under it *. The terms, in which the sale of a patent to Mr. Hine were communicated to the public, naturally called for a parliamentary enquiry. The integrity of the house of commons was directly impeached; but they had not courage to move in

* The examination of this firm, honest man, is printed for *Almon*. The reader will find it a most curious, and a most interesting tract. Doctor Musgrave, with no other support but truth, and his own firmness, resisted, and overcame the whole house of commons.

their own vindication, becauſe the enquiry would have been fatal to Colonel Burgoyne, and the Duke of Grafton. When Sir George Savile branded them with the name of traitors to their conſtituents, when the Lord Mayor, the Sheriffs, and Mr. Trecothick, expreſsly avowed and maintained every part of the city remonſtrance, why did they tamely ſubmit to be inſulted? Why did they not immediately expel thoſe refractory members? Conſcious of the motives, on which they had acted, they prudently preferred infamy to danger, and were better prepared to meet the contempt, than to rouze the indignation of the whole people. Had they expelled thoſe five members, the conſequences of the new doctrine of incapacitation would have come immediately home to every man. The truth of it would then have been fairly tried, without any reference to Mr. Wilkes's private character, or the dignity of the houſe, or the obſtinacy of one particular county. Theſe topics, I know, have had their weight with men, who affecting a character of moderation, in reality conſult nothing but their own immediate eaſe;—who are weak enough to acquieſce under a flagrant violation of the laws,

laws, when it does not directly touch themselves, and care not what injustice is practised upon a man, whose moral character they piously think themselves obliged to condemn. In any other circumstances, the house of commons must have forfeited all credit and dignity, if, after such gross provocation, they had permitted those five gentlemen to sit any longer among them. We should then have seen and felt the operation of a precedent, which is represented to be perfectly barren and harmless. But there is a set of men in this country, whose understandings measure the violation of law, by the magnitude of the instance, not by the important consequences, which flow directly from the principle, and the minister, I presume, did not think it safe to quicken their apprehensions too soon. Had Mr. Hampden reasoned and acted like the moderate men of these days, instead of hazarding his whole fortune in a law-suit with the crown, he would have quietly paid the twenty shillings demanded of him,—the Stuart family would probably have continued upon the throne, and, at this moment, the imposition of ship-money would have been an acknowledged prerogative of the crown.

WHAT then has been the buſineſs of the ſeſſion, after voting the ſupplies, and confirming the determination of the Middleſex election? The extraordinary prorogation of the Iriſh parliament, and the juſt diſcontents of that kingdom, have been paſſed by without notice. Neither the general ſituation of our Colonies, nor that particular diſtreſs which forced the inhabitants of Boſton to take up arms in their defence, have been thought worthy of a moment's conſideration. In the repeal of thoſe acts, which were moſt offenſive to America, the parliament have done every thing, but remove the offence. They have relinguiſhed the revenue, but judiciouſly taken care to preſerve the contention. It is not pretended that the continuation of the tea duty is to produce any direct benefit whatſoever to the mother country. What is it then but an odious, unprofitable exertion of a ſpeculative right, and fixing a badge of ſlavery upon the Americans, without ſervice to their maſters? But it has pleaſed God to give us a mia miniſtry and a parliament, who are neither to be perſuaded by argument, nor inſtructed by experience.

LORD North, I preſume, will not claim an extraordinary merit from any thing he has done this year in the improvement or application of the revenue. A great operation, directed to an important object, though it ſhould fail of ſucceſs, marks the genius and elevates the character of a miniſter. A poor contracted underſtanding deals in little ſchemes, which diſhonour him if they fail, and do him no credit when they ſucceed. Lord North had fortunately the means in his poſſeſſion of reducing all the four per cents at once. The failure of his firſt enterprize in finance is not half ſo diſgraceful to his reputation as a miniſter, as the enterprize itſelf is injurious to the public. Inſtead of ſtriking one deciſive blow, which would have cleared the market at once, upon terms proportioned to the price of the four per cents ſix weeks ago, he has tampered with a pitiful portion of a commodity, which ought never to have been touched but in groſs;—he has given notice to the holders of that ſtock, of a deſign formed by government to prevail upon them to ſurrender it by degrees, conſequently has warned them to hold up and inhance the price;—ſo that the plan of reducing the four per cents muſt either be dropped entirely, or continued with an increaſing diſadvantage to the public. The miniſter's ſagacity has ſerved to raiſe the value of the thing he means to purchaſe, and to ſink that of the three per cents, which it is his purpoſe to ſell. In effect, he has contrived to make it the intereſt of the proprietor of four per cents to ſell out and buy three per cents in the market, rather than ſubſcribe his ſtock upon any terms, that can poſſibly be offered by government.

THE ſtate of the nation leads us naturally to conſider the ſituation of the King. The prorogation of parliament has the effect of a temporary diſſolution. The odium of meaſures adopted by the collective body ſits lightly upon the ſeparate members, who compoſed it. They retire into ſummer quarters, and reſt from the diſgraceful labours of the campaign. But as for the Sovereign, *it is not ſo with him*. HE has a permanent exiſtence in this country; HE cannot withdraw himſelf from the complaints, the discontents, the reproaches of his subjects. They pursue him to his retirement, and invade his domestic happiness, when no address can be obtained from an obsequious parliament to encourage or console him. In other times, the interest of the King and people of England was, as it ought to be, entirely the same. A new system has not only been adopted in fact, but professed upon principle. Ministers are no longer the public servants of the state, but the private domestics of the Sovereign. * One particular class of men are permitted to call themselves the King's friends, as if the body of the people were the King's enemies; or as if his Majesty looked for a resource or consolation, in the attachment of a few favourites, against the general contempt and detestation of his subjects. Edward, and Richard the second, made the same distinction between the collective body of the people, and a contemptible party who surrounded the throne. The event

* "An ignorant, mercenary, and servile crew; unanimous "in evil, diligent in mischief, variable in principles, constant "to flattery, talkers for liberty, but slaves to power;---stiling "themselves the court party, and the prince's only friends."

Davenant.

of

of their miſtaken conduct might have been a warning to their ſucceſſors. Yet the errors of thoſe princes were not without excuſe. They had as many falſe friends, as our preſent gracious Sovereign, and infinitely greater temptations to ſeduce them. They were neither ſober, religious, nor demure. Intoxicated with pleaſure, they waſted their inheritance in purſuit of it. Their lives were like a rapid torrent, brilliant in proſpect, though uſeleſs or dangerous in its courſe. In the dull, unanimated exiſtence of other princes, we ſee nothing but a ſickly, ſtagnant water, which taints the atmoſphere without fertilizing the ſoil.—The morality of a King is not to be meaſured by vulgar rules. His ſituation is ſingular. There are faults which do him honour, and virtues that diſgrace him. A faultleſs, inſipid equality in his character, is neither capable of vice nor virtue in the extreme; but it ſecures his ſubmiſſion to thoſe perſons, whom he has been accuſtomed to reſpect, and makes him a dangerous inſtrument of *their* ambition. Secluded from the world, attached from his infancy to one ſet of perſons, and one ſet of ideas, he can neither open his heart to new connexions, nor his

his mind to better information. A character of this sort is the soil fittest to produce that obstinate bigotry in politics and religion, which begins with a meritorious sacrifice of the understanding, and finally conducts the monarch and the martyr to the block.

At any other period, I doubt not, the scandalous disorders, which have been introduced into the government of all the dependencies in the Empire, would have rouzed the attention of the public. The odious abuse and prostitution of the prerogative at home,—the unconstitutional employment of the military,—the arbitrary fines and commitments by the house of lords, and court of king's bench;—the mercy of a chaste and pious Prince extended chearfully to a wilful murderer, because that murderer is the brother of a common prostitute *, would, I think, at any other time, have excited universal indignation. But the daring attack upon the constitution, in the Middlesex election, makes us callous and indifferent to inferior grievances. No man regards an eruption upon the surface, when the noble parts are invaded, and he

* Miss Kennedy.

feels

feels a mortification approaching to his heart. The free election of our representatives in parliament comprehends, because it is, the source and security of every right and privilege of the English nation. The ministry have realised the compendious ideas of Caligula. They know that the liberty, the laws, and property of an Englishman have in truth but one neck, and that to violate the freedom of election strikes deeply at them all.

JUNIUS.

LETTER XL.

TO LORD NORTH.

MY LORD, 22. *Aug.* 1770.

MR. Luttrell's services were the chief support and ornament of the Duke of Grafton's administration. The honour of rewarding them was reserved for your Lordship. The Duke, it seems, had contracted an obligation he was ashamed to acknowledge, and unable to acquit. You, my Lord, had no scruples. You accepted the succession with all its incumbrances, and have paid Mr. Luttrell his legacy, at the hazard of ruining the estate.

WHEN

When this accomplished youth declared himself the champion of government, the world was busy in enquiring what honours or emoluments could be a sufficient recompence, to a young man of his rank and fortune, for submitting to mark his entrance into life with the universal contempt and detestation of his country.—His noble father had not been so precipitate.—To vacate his seat in parliament;—to intrude upon a county in which he had no interest or connexion;—to possess himself of another man's right, and to maintain it in defiance of public shame as well as justice, bespoke a degree of zeal or of depravity, which all the favour of a pious Prince could hardly requite. I protest, my Lord, there is in this young man's conduct, a strain of prostitution, which, for its singularity, I cannot but admire. He has discovered a new line in the human character;—he has degraded even the name of Luttrell, and gratified his father's most sanguine expectations.

The Duke of Grafton, with every possible disposition to patronise this kind of merit, was contented with pronouncing Colonel Luttrell's

Luttrell's panegyric. The gallant ſpirit, the diſintereſted zeal of the young adventurer, were ecchoed through the houſe of lords. His Grace repeatedly pledged himſelf to the houſe, as an evidence of the purity of his friend Mr. Luttrell's intentions;—that he had engaged without any proſpect of perſonal benefit, and that the idea of compenſation would mortally offend him *. The noble Duke could hardly be in earneſt; but he had lately quitted his employment, and began to think it neceſſary to take ſome care of his reputation. At that very moment the Iriſh negociation was probably begun.—Come forward, thou worthy repreſentative of Lord Bute, and tell this inſulted country, who adviſed the King to appoint Mr. Luttrell, ADJUTANT-GENERAL to the army in Ireland. By what management was Colonel Cuninghame prevailed on to reſign his employment, and the obſequious Giſborne to accept of a penſion for the government of Kinſale †? Was

* He now ſays that his great object is the rank of Colonel, and that he *will* have it.

† This infamous tranſaction ought to be explained to the public. Colonel Giſborne was quarter-maſter-general in Ireland. Lord Townſhend perſuades him to reſign to a Scotch officer,

Was it an original ſtipulation with the Princeſs of Wales, or does he owe his preferment to your Lordſhip's partiality, or to the Duke of Bedford's friendſhip? My Lord, though it may not be poſſible to trace this meaſure to its ſource, we can follow the ſtream, and warn the country of its approaching deſtruction. The Engliſh nation muſt be rouzed, and put upon its guard. Mr. Luttrell has already ſhewn us how far he may be truſted, whenever an open attack is to be made upon the liberties of this country. I do not doubt that there is a deliberate plan formed.——Your Lordſhip beſt knows by whom;—the corruption of the legiſlative body on this ſide—a military force on the other—and then, *Farewell to England!* It is impoſſible that any miniſter ſhall dare to adviſe the King to place ſuch a man as Luttrell in the confidential

officer, one Fraſer, and gives him the government of Kinſale. ---Colonel Cuninghame was Adjutant-general in Ireland. Lord Townſhend offers him a penſion, to induce him to reſign to Luttrell. Cuninghame treats the offer with contempt. What's to be done? poor Giſborne muſt move once more.---He accepts of a penſion of 500 l. a year, until a government of greater value ſhall become vacant. Colonel Cuninghame is made Governor of Kinſale; and Luttrell, at laſt, for whom the whole machinery is put in motion, becomes Adjutant-general, and in effect takes the command of the army in Ireland.

post of Adjutant-general, if there were not some secret purpose in view, which only such a man as Luttrell is fit to promote. The insult offered to the army in general is as gross as the outrage intended to the people of England. What! Lieutenant-colonel Luttrell, Adjutant-general of an army of sixteen thousand men! one would think his Majesty's campaigns at Blackheath and Wimbledon might have taught him better. ——I cannot help wishing General Harvey joy of a colleague, who does so much honour to the employment.—But, my Lord, this measure is too daring to pass unnoticed, too dangerous to be received with indifference or submission. You shall not have time to new-model the Irish army. They will not submit to be garbled by Colonel Luttrell. As a mischief to the English constitution, (for he is not worth the name of enemy) they already detest him. As a boy, impudently thrust over their heads, they will receive him with indignation and contempt.—As for you, my Lord, who perhaps are no more than the blind, unhappy instrument of Lord Bute and her Royal Highness the Princess of Wales, be assured that you shall be called upon to answer for the advice, which has been given, and either diſcover your accomplices, or fall a ſacrifice to their ſecurity.

JUNIUS.

LETTER XLI.

TO THE RIGHT HONOURABLE LORD MANSFIELD.

MY LORD, 14. *November* 1770

THE appearance of this letter will attract the curioſity of the public, and command even your Lordſhip's attention. I am conſiderably in your debt, and ſhall endeavour, once for all, to balance the account. Accept of this addreſs, my Lord, as a prologue to more important ſcenes, in which you will probably be called upon to act or ſuffer.

You will not queſtion my veracity, when I aſſure you that it has not been owing to any particular reſpect for your perſon that I have abſtained from you ſo long. Beſides the diſtreſs and danger with which the preſs is threatened, when your lordſhip is party, and the party is to be judge, I confeſs I have been deterred by the difficulty of the taſk. Our language has no term of reproach, the mind has no idea of deteſtation, which has not already been happily applied to you, and exhauſted.—Ample juſtice has been done by abler pens than mine to the ſeparate merits of your life and character. Let it be *my* humble office to collect the ſcattered ſweets, till their united virtue tortures the ſenſe

PERMIT me to begin with paying a juſt tribute to Scotch ſincerity, wherever I find it. I own I am not apt to confide in the profeſſions of gentlemen of that country, and when they ſmile, I feel an involuntary emotion to guard myſelf againſt miſchief. With this general opinion of an ancient nation, I always thought it much to your lordſhip's honour, that, in your earlier days, you were but little infected with the prudence of your country. You had ſome original attachments, which you took every proper opportunity to acknowledge. The liberal ſpirit of youth prevailed over your native diſcretion.

diſcretion. Your zeal in the cauſe of an unhappy prince was expreſſed with the ſincerity of wine, and ſome of the ſolemnities of religion.* This I conceive, is the moſt amiable point of view, in which your character has appeared. Like an honeſt man, you took that part in politics, which might have been expected from your birth, education, country and connexions. There was ſomething generous in your attachment to the baniſhed houſe of Stuart. We lament the miſtakes of a good man, and do not begin to deteſt him until he affects to renounce his principles. Why did you not adhere to that loyalty you once profeſſed? Why did you not follow the example of your worthy brother? ‡ With him, you might have ſhared in the honour of the Pretender's confidence—with him, you might have preſerved the integrity of your character, and England, I think, might have ſpared you without re-

* THIS man was always a rank Jacobite. Lord Ravenſworth produced the moſt ſatisfactory Evidence of his having frequently drank the Pretender's health upon his knees.

‡ CONFIDENTIAL Secretary to the late Pretender. This circumſtance confirmed the friendſhip between the brothers.

gret. Your friends will say, perhaps, that altho' you deserted the fortune of your liege Lord, you have adhered firmly to the principles which drove his father from the throne;—that without openly supporting the person, you have done essential service to the cause, and consoled yourself for the loss of a favourite family by reviving and establishing the maxims of their government. This is the way, in which a Scotchman's understanding corrects the error of his heart.—My lord, I acknowledge the truth of the defence, and can trace it through all your conduct. I see through your whole life, one uniform plan to enlarge the power of the crown, at the expence of the liberty of the subject. To this object, your thoughts, words and actions have been constantly directed. In contempt or ignorance of the common law of England, you have made it your study to introduce into the court, where you preside, maxims of jurisprudence unknown to Englishmen. The Roman code, the law of nations, and the opinion of foreign civilians, are your perpetual theme;—but whoever heard you mention Magna Charta or the Bill of Rights with approbation or respect? By such trea-

treacherous arts, the noble ſimplicity and free ſpirit of our Saxon laws were firſt corrupted. The Norman conqueſt was not compleat, until Norman lawyers had introduced their laws, and reduced ſlavery to a ſyſtem.—This one leading principle directs your interpretation of the laws, and accounts for your treatment of juries. It is not in political queſtions only (for there the courtier might be forgiven) but let the cauſe be what it may, your underſtanding is equally on the rack, either to contract the power of the jury, or to miſlead their judgment. For the truth of this aſſertion, I appeal to the doctrine you delivered in Lord Groſvenor's cauſe. An action for criminal converſation being brought by a peer againſt a prince of the blood, you were daring enough to tell the jury that, in fixing the damages, they were to pay no regard to the quality or fortune of the parties;—that it was a trial between A. and B.—that they were to conſider the offence in a moral light only, and give no greater damages to a peer of the realm, than to the meaneſt mechanic. I ſhall not attempt to refute a doctrine, which, if it was meant for law, carries falſhood and abſurdity upon the face of it; but, if it was meant for a declaration of your political creed, is clear and consistent. Under an arbitrary government, all ranks and distinctions are confounded. The honour of a nobleman is no more considered than the reputation of a peasant, for, with different liveries, they are equally slaves.

EVEN in matters of private property, we see the same byass and inclination to depart from the decisions of your predecessors, which you certainly ought to receive as evidence of the common law. Instead of those certain, positive rules, by which the judgment of a court of law should invariably be determined, you have fondly introduced your own unsettled notions of equity and substantial justice. Decisions given upon such principles do not alarm the public so much as they ought, because the consequence and tendency of each particular instance, is not observed or regarded. In the mean time the practice gains ground; the court of King's Bench becomes a court of equity, and the judge, instead of consulting strictly the law of the land, refers only to the wisdom of the court,

court, and to the purity of his own conſcience. The name of Mr. Juſtice Yates, will naturally revive in your mind ſome of thoſe emotions of fear and deteſtation, with which you always beheld him. That great lawyer, that honeſt man, ſaw your whole conduct in the light that I do. After years of ineffectual reſiſtance to the pernicious principles introduced by your Lordſhip, and uniformly ſupported by your *humble friends* upon the bench, he determined, to quit a court, whoſe proceedings and deciſions he could neither aſſent to with honour, nor oppoſe with ſucceſs.

* THE injuſtice done to an Individual is ſometimes of ſervice to the public. Facts are apt to alarm us more than the moſt dangerous principles. The ſufferings and firmneſs of a Printer have rouſed the public attention. You knew and felt that your conduct would not bear a parliamentary inquiry, and you hoped to eſcape it by the meaneſt, the baſeſt ſacrifice of dignity and conſiſtency,

* THE oppreſſion of an obſcure individual gave birth to the famous *Habeas Corpus* Act of 31. Car. 2. which is frequently conſidered as another Magna Charta of the Kingdom. *Blackſtone*, 3. 135.

 that

that ever was made by a great magiſtrate. Where was your firmneſs, where was that vindictive ſpirit, of which we have ſeen ſo many examples, when a man, ſo inconſiderable as Bingley, could force you to confeſs, in the face of this country, that, for two years together, you had illegally deprived an Engliſh ſubject of his liberty, and that he had triumphed over you at laſt? Yet I own, my lord, that your's is not an uncommon character. Women, and men like women, are timid, vindictive, and irreſolute. Their paſſions counteract each other, and make the ſame creature, at one moment hateful, at another contemptible. I fancy, my Lord, ſome time will elapſe before you venture to commit another Engliſhman for refuſing to anſwer interrogatories. †

THE doctrine you have conſtantly delivered, in caſes of libel, is another powerful

† BINGLEY was committed for contempt in not ſubmitting to be examined: He lay in priſon two years, until the Crown thought the matter might occaſion ſome ſerious complaint, and therefore he was let out, in the ſame contumelious ſtate he had been put in, with all his ſins about him, unannointed and unannealed.---There was much coquetry between the Court and the Attorney General, about who ſhould undergo the ridicule of letting him eſcape.---*Vide another Letter to* ALMON, *p.* 189.

evidence

evidence of a ſettled plan to contract the legal power of juries, and to draw queſtions, inſeparable from fact, within the *arbitrium* of the court.. Here, my Lord, you have fortune of your ſide. When you invade the province of the jury, in matter of libel, you, in effect, attack the liberty of the preſs, and with a ſingle ſtroke, wound two of your greateſt enemies.—In ſome inſtances you have ſucceeded, becauſe jurymen are too often ignorant of their own rights, and too apt to be awed by the authority of a chief juſtice. In other criminal proſecutions, the malice of the deſign is confeſſedly as much the ſubject of conſideration to a jury, as the certainty of the fact. If a different doctrine prevails in the caſe of libels, why ſhould it not extend to *all* criminal caſes?—Why not to capital offences? I ſee no reaſon (and I dare ſay you will agree with me that there is no good one) why the life of the ſubject ſhould be better protected againſt you, than his liberty or property. Why ſhould you enjoy the full power of pillory, fine, and impriſonment, and not be indulged with hanging or tranſportation? With your Lordſhip's fertile genius and merciful diſpoſition, I can conceive ſuch an exercise of the power you have, as could hardly be aggravated by that which you have not.

But, my Lord, since you have laboured, (and not unsuccessfully) to destroy the substance *of the trial*, why should you suffer the form of the *verdict* to remain? Why force twelve honest men, in palpable violation of their oaths, to pronounce their fellow-subject a *guilty* man, when, almost at the same moment, you forbid their enquiring into the only circumstance, which in the eye of law and reason, constitutes guilt—the malignity or innocence of his intentions?—But I understand your Lordship.—If you could succeed in making the trial by jury useless and ridiculous, you might then with greater safety introduce a bill into parliament for enlarging the jurisdiction of the court, and extending your favourite trial by interrogatories to every question, in which the life or liberty of an Englishman is concerned. *

Your

* The philosophical poet, doth notably describe the damnable and damned proceedings of the Judge of Hell,

'Gnossius hæc Rhadamanthus habet durissima regna,
"Castigatque, auditque dolos, *subigitque fateri*."

First he punisheth, and *then* he heareth: and lastly compelleth to confess, and makes and mars laws at his pleasure; like

Your charge to the jury, in the proſecution againſt Almon and Woodfall, contradicts the higheſt legal authorities, as well as the plaineſt dictates of reaſon. In Miller's cauſe, and ſtill more expreſsly in that of Baldwin, you have proceeded a ſtep farther, and groſsly contradicted yourſelf.—You may know perhaps, though I do not mean to inſult you by an appeal to your experience, that the language of truth is uniform and conſiſtent. To depart from it ſafely, requires memory and diſcretion. In the two laſt trials, your charge to the jury began, as uſual, with aſſuring them that they had nothing to do with the law,—that they were to find the bare fact, and not concern themſelves about the legal inferences drawn from it, or the degree of the defendant's guilt. —Thus far you were conſiſtent with your former practice.—But how will you account for the concluſion? You told the jury that, "if, after all, they would take upon them-

like as the Centurion, in the holy hiſtory did to St. Paul, for the text ſaith, "Centurio apprehendi Paulum juſſit, & ſe "catenis eligari, et *tunc* INTERROGABAT, quis fuiſſet, & "quid feciſſet;" but good Judges and Juſtices abhor theſe Courſes. *Coke* 2. *Inſt*. 55.

" ſelves to determine the law, *they might do* " *it*, but they muſt be very ſure that they " determined according to law, for it touch- " ed their conſciences, and they acted at " their peril."—If I underſtand your firſt propoſition, you meant to affirm, that the jury were not competent judges of the law in the criminal caſe of a libel—that it did not fall within *their* juriſdiction; and that, with reſpect to *them*, the malice or innocence of the defendants intentions would be a queſtion *coram non judice*.—But the ſecond propoſition clears away your own difficulties, and reſtores the jury to all their judicial capacities. * You make the competence of the court to depend upon the legality of the deciſion. In the firſt inſtance you deny the power abſolutely. In the ſecond, you admit the power, provided it be legally exerciſed. Now, my Lord, without pretending to reconcile the diſtinctions of Weſtminſter-hall with the ſimple information of common-ſenſe, or the integrity of fair argument, I

* Directly the reverſe of the doctrine he conſtantly maintained in the houſe of lords and elſewhere, upon the deciſion of the Middleſex election. He invariably aſſerted that the deciſion muſt be *legal*, becauſe the court was *competent*; and never could be prevailed on to enter farther into the queſtion.

ſhall

ſhall be underſtood by your Lordſhip, when I aſſert that, if a jury or any other court of judicature (for jurors are judges) have no right to entertain a cauſe, or queſtion of law, it ſignifies nothing whether their deciſion be or be not according to law. Their deciſion is in itſelf a mere nullity: the parties are not bound to ſubmit to it; and, if the jury run any riſque of puniſhment, it is not for pronouncing a corrupt or illegal verdict, but for the illegality of meddling with a point, on which they have no legal authority to decide *.

I CANNOT quit this ſubject without reminding your Lordſhip of the name of Mr. Benſon. Without offering any legal objection, you ordered a ſpecial juryman to be ſet aſide in a cauſe, where the King was proſecutor. The novelty of the fact required explanation. Will you condeſcend to tell the world by what law or cuſtom you were

* Theſe iniquitous proſecutions coſt the beſt of princes ſix thouſand pounds, and ended in the total defeat and diſgrace of the proſecutors. In the courſe of one of them Judge Aſton had the unparallelled impudence to tell Mr. Morris (a gentleman of unqueſtionable honour and integrity, and who was then giving his evidence on oath) that *he ſhould pay very little regard to any affidavit he ſhould make.*

autho-

authoriſed to make a peremptory challenge of a juryman? The parties indeed have this power, and perhaps your Lordſhip, having accuſtomed yourſelf to unite the characters of judge and party, may claim it in virtue of the new capacity you have aſſumed, and profit by your own wrong. The time, within which you might have been puniſhed for this daring attempt to pack a jury, is, I fear, elapſed; but no length of time ſhall eraſe the record of it.

THE miſchiefs you have done this country, are not confined to your interpretation of the laws. You are a miniſter, my Lord, and, as ſuch, have long been conſulted. Let us candidly examine what uſe you have made of your miniſterial influence. I will not deſcend to little matters, but come at once to thoſe important points, on which your reſolution was waited for, on which the expectation of your opinion kept a great part of the nation in ſuſpence.—A conſtitutional queſtion ariſes upon a declaration of the law of parliament, by which the freedom of election, and the birthright of the ſubject were ſuppoſed to have been invaded.--The King's ſervants are accuſed of violating the conſtitution.

tion.—The nation is in a ferment.—The ableſt men of all parties engage in the queſtion, and exert their utmoſt abilities in the diſcuſſion of it.—What part has the honeſt Lord Mansfield acted? As an eminent judge of the law, his opinion would have been reſpected.—As a peer, he had a right to demand an audience of his Sovereign, and inform him that his miniſters were purſuing unconſtitutional meaſures.—Upon other occaſions, my Lord, you have no difficulty in finding your way into the cloſet. The pretended neutrality of belonging to no party, will not ſave your reputation. In queſtions merely political, an honeſt man may ſtand neuter. But the laws and conſtitution are the general property of the ſubject; not to defend is to relinquiſh;—and who is there ſo ſenſeleſs as to renounce his ſhare in a common benefit, unleſs he hopes to profit by a new diviſion of the ſpoil. As a lord of parliament, you were repeatedly called upon to condemn or defend the new law declared by the houſe of commons. You affected to have ſcruples, and every expedient was attempted to remove them.—The queſtion was propoſed and urged to you in a thouſand different ſhapes.—Your prudence ſtill ſupplied you with evaſion;—

your

your refolution was invincible. For my own part, I am not anxious to penetrate this folemn fecret. I care not to whofe wifdom it is intrufted, nor how foon you carry it with you to your grave *. You have betrayed your opinion by the very care you have taken to conceal it. It is not from Lord Mansfield that we expect any referve in declaring his real fentiments in favour of government, or in oppofition to the people; nor is it difficult to account for the motions of a timid, difhoneft heart, which neither has virtue enough to acknowledge truth, nor courage to contradict it.—Yet you continue to fupport an adminiftration which you know is univerfally odious, and which, on fome occafions, you yourfelf fpeak of with contempt. You would fain be thought to take no fhare in government, while, in reality, you are the main fpring of the machine.—Here too we trace the *little*, prudential policy of a Scotchman.---Inftead of acting that open, generous part, which becomes your rank and ftation, you meanly fkulk into the clofet and give your

* He faid in the houfe of lords, that he believed he fhould carry his opinion with him to the grave. It was afterwards reported that he had intrufted it, in fpecial confidence, to the ingenious Duke of Cumberland.

Sove-

Sovereign ſuch advice, as you have not ſpirit to avow or defend. You ſecretly ingroſs the power, while you decline the title of miniſter; and though you dare not be Chancellor, you know how to ſecure the emoluments of the office.—Are the ſeals to be for ever in commiſſion, that you may enjoy five thouſand pounds a year?—I beg pardon, my Lord;—your fears have interpoſed at laſt, and forced you to reſign.—The odium of continuing ſpeaker of the houſe of lords, upon ſuch terms, was too formidable to be reſiſted. What a multitude of bad paſſions are forced to ſubmit to a conſtitutional infirmity! But though you have relinquiſhed the ſalary, you ſtill aſſume the rights of a miniſter.—Your conduct, it ſeems, muſt be defended in parliament.—For what other purpoſe is your wretched friend, that miſerable ſerjeant, poſted to the houſe of commons? Is it in the abilities of Mr. Leigh to defend the great Lord Mansfield?—Or is he only the punch of the puppet-ſhew, to ſpeak as he is prompted, by the CHIEF JUGGLER behind the curtain *?

* This paragraph gagged poor *Leigh*. I really am concerned for the man, and wiſh it were poſſible to open his mouth.—He is a very pretty orator.

In public affairs, my Lord, cunning, let it be ever ſo well wrought, will not conduct a man honourably through life. Like bad money, it may be current for a time, but it will ſoon be cried down. It cannot conſiſt with a liberal ſpirit, though it be ſometimes united with extraordinary qualifications. When I acknowledge your abilities, you may believe I am ſincere. I feel for human nature, when I ſee a man, ſo gifted as you are, deſcend to ſuch vile practiſe.—Yet do not ſuffer your vanity to conſole you too ſoon. Believe me, my good Lord, you are not admired in the ſame degree, in which you are deteſted. It is only the partiality of your friends, that balances the defects of your heart with the ſuperiority of your underſtanding. No learned man, even among your own tribe, thinks you qualified to preſide in a court of common law. Yet it is confeſſed that, under *Juſtinian*, you might have made an incomparable *Prætor*.—It is remarkable enough, but I hope not ominous, that the laws you underſtand beſt, and the judges you affect to admire moſt, flouriſhed in the decline of a great empire, and are ſuppoſed to have contributed to its fall.

HERE,

Here, my Lord, it may be proper for us to pauſe together.—It is not for my own ſake that I wiſh you to conſider the delicacy of your ſituation. Beware how you indulge the firſt emotions of your reſentment. This paper is delivered to the world, and cannot be recalled. The perſecution of an innocent printer cannot alter facts, nor refute arguments.—Do not furniſh me with farther materials againſt yourſelf.—An honeſt man, like the true religion, appeals to the underſtanding, or modeſtly confides in the internal evidence of his conſcience. The impoſtor employs force inſtead of argument, impoſes ſilence where he cannot convince, and propagates his character by the ſword.

JUNIUS.

LETTER XLII.

TO THE PRINTER OF THE PUBLIC ADVERTISER.

SIR, *January* 30, 1771.

IF we recollect in what manthe *King's Friends* have been constantly employed, we shall have no reason to be surprised at any condition of disgrace, to which the once-respected name of Englishmen may be degraded. His Majesty has no cares, but such as concern the laws and constitution of this country. In his Royal breast there is no room left for resentment, no place for hostile sentiments against the natural enemies of his crown. The system of government is uniform.—Violence and oppression at home can only be supported by treachery and submission abroad. When the civil rights of the people are daringly invaded on one side, what have we to to expect, but that their political rights should be deserted and betrayed, in the same proportion, on the other? The plan of domestic policy, which has been invariably pursued, from the moment of his present Majesty's accession, engrosses all the attention of his servants. They know that the security of their places depends upon their maintaining, at any hazard, the secret system of the closet. A foreign war might embarrass, an unfavourable event might ruin the minister, and defeat the deep-laid scheme of policy, to which he and his associates owe their employments. Rather than suffer the execution of that scheme to be delayed or interrupted, the King has been advised to make a public surrender, a solemn sacrifice, in the face of all Europe, not only of the interests of his subjects, but of his own personal reputation, and of the dignity of that crown, which his predecessors have worn with honour. These are strong terms, Sir, but they are supported by fact and argument.

THE King of Great-Britain had been for some years in possession of an island, to which, as the ministry themselves have repeatedly asserted, the Spaniards had no claim of right.

The importance of the place is not in question. If it were, a better judgment might be formed of it from the opinion of Lord Anson and Lord Egmont, and from the anxiety of the Spaniards, than from any fallacious insinuations thrown out by men, whose interest it is to undervalue that property, which they are determined to relinquish. The pretensions of Spain were a subject of negotiation between the two courts. They had been discussed, but not admitted. The King of Spain, in these circumstances, bids adieu to amicable negotiation, and appeals directly to the sword. The expedition against Port Egmont does not appear to have been a sudden ill-concerted enterprise. It seems to have been conducted not only with the usual military precautions, but in all the forms and ceremonies of war. A frigate was first employed to examine the strength of the place. A message was then sent, demanding immediate possession, in the Catholic King's name, and ordering our people to depart. At last a military force appears, and compels the garrison to surrender. A formal capitulation ensues, and his Majesty's ship, which might at least have been permitted to bring home his

his troops immediately, is detained in port twenty days, and her rudder forcibly taken away. This train of facts carries no appearance of the raſhneſs or violence of a Spaniſh governor. On the contrary, the whole plan ſeems to have been formed and executed, in conſequence of deliberate orders, and a regular inſtruction from the Spaniſh court. Mr. Bucarelli is not a pirate, nor has he been treated as ſuch by thoſe who employed him. I feel for the honour of a gentleman, when I affirm that our King owes him a ſignal reparation. —Where will the humiliation of this country end! A King of Great Britain, not contented with placing himſelf upon a level with a Spaniſh governor, deſcends ſo low as to do a notorious injuſtice to that governor. As a ſalvo for his own reputation, he has been adviſed to traduce the character of a brave officer, and to treat him as a common robber, when he knew with certainty that Mr. Bucarelli had acted in obedience to his orders, and had done no more than his duty. Thus it happens in private life, with a man who has no ſpirit nor ſenſe of honour.—One of his equals orders a ſervant to ſtrike him.—Inſtead of returning the blow to the maſter, his courage is contented with throwing an aspersion, equally false and public, upon the character of the servant.

THIS short recapitulation was necessary to introduce the consideration of his Majesty's speech, of 13. November, 1770, and the subsequent measures of government. The excessive caution, with which the speech was drawn up, had impressed upon me an early conviction, that no serious resentment was thought of, and that the conclusion of the business, whenever it happened, must, in some degree, be dishonourable to England. There appears through the whole speech a guard and reserve in the choice of expression, which shews how careful the ministry were not to embarrass their future projects by any firm or spirited declaration from the throne. When all hopes of peace are lost, his Majesty tells his parliament, that he is preparing,—not for barbarous war, but (with all his mother's softness,) *for a different Situation.*—An open hostility, authorised by the Catholic King, is called *an act of a governor.* This act, to avoid the mention of a regular siege and surrender, passes under the piratical description of *seizing by force*;

force; and the thing taken is described, not as a part of the King's territory or proper dominion, but merely as a *possession*, a word expressly chosen in contradistinction to, and exclusion of the idea of *right*, and to prepare us for a future surrender both of the right and of the possession. Yet this speech, Sir, cautious and equivocal as it is, cannot, by any sophistry, be accommodated to the measures, which have since been adopted. It seemed to promise, that whatever might be given up by secret stipulation, some care would be taken to save appearances to the public. The event shews us, that to depart, in the minutest article, from the nicety and strictness of punctilio, is as dangerous to national honour, as to female virtue. The woman, who admits of one familiarity, seldom knows where to stop, or what to refuse; and when the counsels of a great country give way in a single instance,—when they once are inclined to submission, every step accelerates the rapidity of the descent. The ministry themselves, when they framed the speech, did not foresee, that they should ever accede to such an accommodation, as they have since advised their master to accept of.

THE

The King ſays, *The honour of my crown and the rights of my people are deeply affected.* The Spaniard, in his reply, ſays, *I give you back poſſeſſion, but I adhere to my claim of prior right, reſerving the aſſertion of it for a more favourable opportunity.*

The ſpeech ſays, *I made an immediate demand of ſatisfaction, and, if that fails, I am prepared to do myſelf juſtice.* This immediate demand muſt have been ſent to Madrid on the 12th of September, or in a few days after. It was certainly refuſed, or evaded, and the King *has not* done himſelf juſtice.—When the firſt magiſtrate ſpeaks to the nation, ſome care ſhould be taken of his apparent veracity.

The ſpeech proceeds to ſay, *I ſhall not diſcontinue my preparations until I have received proper reparation for the injury.* If this aſſurance may be relied on, what an enormous expence is entailed, *ſine die*, upon this unhappy country! Reſtitution of a poſſeſſion, and reparation of an injury are as different in ſubſtance, as they are in language. The very act of reſtitution may contain, as in this inſtance it palpably does, a ſhameful aggravation

aggravation of the injury. A man of ſpirit does not meaſure the degree of an injury by the mere poſitive damage he has ſuſtained. He conſiders the principle on which it is founded; he reſents the ſuperiority aſſerted over him; and rejects with indignation the claim of right, which his adverſary endeavours to eſtabliſh, and would force him to acknowledge.

THE motives, on which the Catholic King makes reſtitution, are, if poſſible, more inſolent and diſgraceful to our Sovereign, than even the declaratory condition annexed to it. After taking four months to conſider, whether the expedition was undertaken by his own orders or not, he condeſcends to diſavow the enterprize, and to reſtore the iſland,—not from any regard to juſtice;—not from any regard he bears to his Britannic Majeſty, but merely *from the perſuaſion, in which he is, of the pacific ſentiments of the King of Great Britain.*—At this rate, if our King had diſcovered the ſpirit of a man,—if he had made a peremptory demand of ſatisfaction, the King of Spain would have given him a peremptory refuſal. But why this unſeaſonable, this ridiculous mention of the

the King of Great Britain's pacific intentions? Have they ever been in question? Was *He* the aggressor? Does he attack foreign powers without provocation? Does he even resist, when he is insulted? No, Sir, if any ideas of strife or hostility have entered his royal mind, they have a very different direction. The enemies of England have nothing to fear from them.

AFTER all, Sir, to what kind of disavowal has the King of Spain at last consented? Supposing it made in proper time, it should have been accompanied with instant restitution; and if Mr. Bucarelli acted without orders, he deserved death. Now, Sir, instead of immediate restitution, we have a four months negociation, and the officer, whose act is disavowed, returns to court, and is loaded with honours.

IF the actual situation of Europe be considered, the treachery of the King's servants, particularly of Lord North, who takes the whole upon himself, will appear in the strongest colours of aggravation. Our allies were masters of the Mediterranean. The King of France's present aversion from war, and the distraction

distraction of his affairs are notorious. He is now in a state of war with his people. In vain did the Catholic King solicit him to take part in the quarrel against us. His finances were in the last disorder, and it was probable that his troops might find sufficient employment at home. In these circumstances, we might have dictated the law to Spain. There are no terms, to which she might not have been compelled to submit. At the worst, a war with Spain alone, carries the fairest promise of advantage. One good effect at least would have been immediately produced by it. The desertion of France would have irritated her ally, and in all probability have dissolved the family compact. The scene is now fatally changed. The advantage is thrown away. The most favourable opportunity is lost.—Hereafter we shall know the value of it. When the French King is reconciled to his subjects; when Spain has compleated her preparations; when the collected strength of the house of Bourbon attacks us at once, the King himself will be able to determine upon the wisdom or imprudence of his present conduct. As far as the probability of argument extends, we may safely pronounce, that a conjuncture, which threatens

threatens the very being of this country, has been wilfully prepared and forwarded by our own miniſtry. How far the people may be animated to reſiſtance under the preſent adminiſtration, I know not; but this I know with certainty, that, under the preſent adminiſtration, or if any thing like it ſhould continue, it is of very little moment whether we are a conquered nation or not*.

HAVING travelled thus far in the high road of matter of fact, I may now be permitted to wander a little into the field of imagination. Let us baniſh from our minds the

* The King's acceptance of the Spaniſh Ambaſſador's declaration, is drawn up in barbarous French, and ſigned by the Earl of Rochford. This diplomatic Lord has ſpent his life in the ſtudy and practice of *Etiquettes*, and is ſuppoſed to be a profound maſter of the ceremonies. I will not inſult him by any reference to grammar or common ſenſe, if he were even acquainted with the common forms of his office, I ſhould think him as well qualified for it, as any man in his Majeſty's ſervice.----The reader is requeſted to obſerve Lord Rochford's method of authenticating a public inſtrument. "En foi de "quoi, *moi* ſouſſigné, un des principaux Secretaires d'Etat "S. M. B. *ai* ſigné la preſente de ma ſignature ordinaire, et "icelle fait appoſer le cachet de *nos* Armes." In three lines there are no leſs than ſeven falſe concords. But the man does not even know the ſtile of his office;---If he had known it, he would have ſaid "*nous*, ſouſſigné Secretaire "d'Etat de S. M. B. avons ſigné *&c.*"

per-

persuasion that these events have really happened in the reign of the best of princes. Let us consider them as nothing more than the materials of a fable, in which we may conceive the Sovereign of some other country to be concerned. I mean to violate all the laws of probability, when I suppose that this imaginary King, after having voluntarily disgraced himself in the eyes of his subjects, might return to a sense of his dishonour;—that he might perceive the snare laid for him by his ministers, and feel a spark of shame kindling in his breast.—The part he must then be obliged to act, would overwhelm him with confusion. To his parliament he must say, *I called you together to receive your advice, and have never asked your opinion.*—To the merchant,—*I have distressed your commerce; I have dragged your seamen out of your ships, I have loaded you with a grievous weight of insurances.*—To the landholder,—*I told you war was too probable, when I was determined to submit to any terms of accommodation; I extorted new taxes from you before it was possible they could be wanted, and am now unable to account for the application of them.*—To the public creditor,—*I have delivered up your fortunes a prey to foreigners and to the vilest of your fellow*

subjects.

ſubjects. Perhaps this repenting Prince might conclude with one general acknowledgement to them all,—*I have involved every rank of my ſubjects in anxiety and diſtreſs, and have nothing to offer you in return, but the certainty of national diſhonour, an armed truce, and peace without ſecurity.*

If theſe accounts were ſettled, there would ſtill remain an apology to be made to his navy and to his army. To the firſt he would ſay, *you were once the terror of the world. But go back to your harbours. A man diſhonoured, as I am, has no uſe for your ſervice.* It is not probable that he would appear again before his ſoldiers, even in the pacific ceremony of a review*. But wherever he appeared, the humiliating confeſſion would be extorted from him. *I have received a blow,—and had not ſpirit to reſent it. I demanded ſatisfaction, and have accepted a declaration, in which the right to ſtrike me again is aſſerted and confirmed.* His countenance at leaſt would ſpeak this language, and even his guards would bluſh for him.

* A Miſtake. He appears before them every day, with the mark of a blow upon his face.---*proh pudor!*

But

BUT to return to our argument.—The miniſtry, it ſeems, are labouring to draw a line of diſtinction between the honour of the crown and the rights of the people. This new idea has yet been only ſtarted in diſcourſe, for in effect both objects have been equally ſacrificed. I neither underſtand the diſtinction, nor what uſe the miniſtry propoſe to make of it. The King's honour is that of his people. *Their* real honour and real intereſt are the ſame.—I am not contending for a vain punctilio. A clear, unblemiſhed character comprehends not only the integrity that will not offer, but the ſpirit that will not ſubmit to an injury; and whether it belongs to an individual or to a community, it is the foundation of peace, of independance, and of ſafety. Private credit is wealth;—public honour is ſecurity.—The feather that adorns the royal bird, ſupports his flight. Strip him of his plumage and you fix him to the earth.

JUNIUS.

LETTER XLIII.

TO THE PRINTER OF THE PUBLIC ADVERTISER.

SIR, 6. *February*, 1771

I HOPE your correſpondent *Junius* is better employed than in anſwering or reading the criticiſms of a news-paper. This is a taſk, from which, if he were inclined to ſubmit to it, his friends ought to relieve him. Upon this principle, I ſhall undertake to anſwer Anti-Junius; more, I believe, to his conviction than to his ſatisfaction. Not daring to attack the main body of *Junius*'s laſt letter, he triumphs in having, as he thinks, ſurpriſed an out-poſt, and cut off a detached argument, a mere ſtraggling propoſition. But even in this petty warfare, he ſhall find himſelf defeated.

JUNIUS does not ſpeak of the Spaniſh *nation* as the *natural enemies* of England. He applies that deſcription with the ſtricteſt truth and juſtice, to the Spaniſh *Court*. From the

the moment, when a Prince of the House of Bourbon ascended that throne, their whole system of government was inverted and became hostile to this country. Unity of possession introduced a unity of politics, and Lewis the fourteenth had reason when he said to his grandson, "*The Pyrenees are removed.*" The History of the present century is one continued confirmation of the phrophecy.

THE Assertion "*That violence and oppression at home can only be supported by treachery and submission abroad,*" is applied to a free people, whose rights are invaded, not to the government of a country, where despotic, or absolute power is confessedly vested in the prince; and with this application, the assertion is true. An absolute monarch having no points to carry at home, will naturally maintain the honour of his crown in all his transactions with foreign powers. But if we could suppose the Sovereign of a free nation, possessed with a design to make himself absolute, he would be inconsistent with himself if he suffered his projects to be interrupted or embarrassed by a foreign war; unless that war tended, as in some cases it might, to promote his principal design. Of the three exceptions

tions to this general rule of conduct, (quoted by Anti-Junius) that of Oliver Cromwell is the only one in point. Harry the Eighth, by the submission of his parliament, was as absolute a prince as Lewis the Fourteenth. Queen Elizabeth's government was not oppressive to the people; and as to her foreign wars, it ought to be considered that they were *unavoidable*. The national honour was not in question. She was compelled to fight in defence of her own person and of her title to the crown. In the common cause of selfish policy, Oliver Cromwell should have cultivated the friendship of foreign powers, or at least have avoided disputes with them, the better to establish his tyranny at home. Had he been only a bad man, he would have sacrificed the honour of the nation to the success of his domestic policy. But, with all his crimes, he had the spirit of an Englishman. The conduct of such a man must always be an exception to vulgar rules. He had abilities sufficient to reconcile contradictions, and to make a great nation at the same moment unhappy and formidable. If it were not for the respect I bear the minister, I could name a man, who, without one grain of understanding, can do half as much as Oliver Cromwell.

WHE-

WHETHER or no there be a *ſecret ſyſtem* in the cloſet, and what may be the object of it, are queſtions, which can only be determined by appearances, and on which every man muſt decide for himſelf.

THE whole plan of *Junius*'s letter proves that he himſelf makes no diſtinction between the real honour of the crown and the real intereſt of the people. In the climax, to which your correſpondent objects, *Junius* adopts the language of the Court, and, by that conformity, gives ſtrength to his argument. He ſays that, " *the King has not only ſacrificed the* " *intereſts of his people, but,* (what was likely " to touch him more nearly,) *his perſonal re-* " *putation and the dignity of his crown.*"

THE queries, put by *Anti-Junius*, can only be anſwered by the miniſtry. Abandoned as they are, I fancy they will not confeſs that they have for ſo many years, maintained poſſeſſion of another man's property. After admitting the aſſertion of the miniſtry —viz. *that the Spaniards had no rightful claim*, and after juſtifying them for ſaying ſo;—it is *his* buſineſs not *mine*, to give us ſome good

 reaſon

reason for their *suffering the pretensions of Spain to be a subject of negotiation.* He admits the facts;—let him reconcile them if he can.

THE last paragraph brings us back to the original question, whether the Spanish declaration contains such a satisfaction as the King of Great Britain ought to have accepted. This was the field, upon which he ought to have encountered *Junius* openly and fairly. But here he leaves the argument, as no longer defensible. I shall therefore conclude with one general admonition to my fellow subjects;—that, when they hear these matters debated, they should not suffer themselves to be misled by general declamations upon the conveniences of peace, or the miseries of war. Between peace and war, abstractedly, there is not, there cannot be a question in the mind of a rational being. The real questions are, *Have we any security that the peace we have so dearly purchased will last a twelvemonth?* and, if not,—*have we, or have we not, sacrificed the fairest opportunity of making war with advantage?*

PHILO JUNIUS.

LET-

LETTER XLIV.

TO THE PRINTER OF THE PUBLIC ADVERTISER.

SIR, 22. *April* 1771.

TO write for profit without taxing the preſs;—to write for fame and to be unknown;—to ſupport the intrigues of faction and to be diſowned, as a dangerous auxiliary, by every party in the kingdom, are contradictions, which the miniſter muſt reconcile, before I forfeit my credit with the public. I may quit the ſervice, but it would be abſurd to ſuſpect me of deſertion. The reputation of theſe papers is an honourable pledge for my attachment to the people. To ſacrifice a reſpected character, and to renounce the eſteem of ſociety, requires more than Mr. Wedderburne's reſolution; and though, in him, it was rather a profeſſion than a deſertion of his principles, [I ſpeak tenderly of this gentleman, for when treachery is in queſtion, I think we ſhould make allowances for a Scotchman,] yet we have ſeen him in the houſe of commons overwhelmed with confusion, and almost bereft of his faculties.—But in truth, Sir, I have left no room for an accommodation with the piety of St. James's. My offences are not to be redeemed by recantation or repentance. On one side, our warmest patriots would disclaim me as a burthen to their honest ambition. On the other, the vilest prostitution, if *Junius* could descend to it, would lose its natural merit and influence in the cabinet, and treachery be no longer a recommendation to the royal favour.

The persons, who, till within these few years, have been most distinguished by their zeal for high church and prerogative, are now, it seems, the great assertors of the privileges of the house of commons. This sudden alteration of their sentiments or language carries with it a suspicious appearance. When I hear the undefined privileges of the popular branch of the legislature exalted by Tories and Jacobites, at the expence of those strict rights, which are known to the subject and limited by the laws, I cannot but suspect, that some mischievous scheme is in agitation, to destroy both law and privilege, by opposing them to each other.

other. They who have uniformly denied the power of the whole legislature to alter the descent of the crown, and whose ancestors, in rebellion against his Majesty's family, have defended that doctrine at the hazard of their lives, now tell us that privilege of parliament is the only rule of right, and the chief security of the public freedom.—I fear, Sir, that, while forms remain, there has been some material change in the substance of our constitution. The opinions of these men were too absurd to be so easily renounced. Liberal minds are open to conviction.—Liberal doctrines are capable of improvement.—There are proselites from atheism, but none from superstition.—If their present professions were sincere, I think they could not but be highly offended at seeing a question, concerning parliamentary privilege, unnecessarily started at a season so unfavourable to the house of commons, and by so very mean and insignificant a person as the minor *Onslow*. They knew that the present house of commons, having commenced hostilities with the people, and degraded the authority of the laws by their own example, were likely enough to be resisted, *per fas & nefas*. If they were really friends to privilege, they would

would have thought the queſtion of right too dangerous to be hazarded at this ſeaſon, and, without the formality of a convention, would have left it undecided.

I HAVE been ſilent hitherto, though not from that ſhameful indifference about the intereſts of ſociety, which too many of us profeſs, and call moderation. I confeſs, Sir, that I felt the prejudices of my education, in favour of a houſe of commons, ſtill hanging about me. I thought that a queſtion, between law and privilege, could never be brought to a formal deciſion, without inconvenience to the public ſervice, or a manifeſt diminution of legal liberty;—that it ought therefore to be carefully avoided: and when I ſaw that the violence of the houſe of commons had carried them too far to retreat, I determined not to deliver a haſty opinion upon a matter of ſo much delicacy and importance.

THE ſtate of things is much altered in this country, ſince it was neceſſary to protect our repreſentatives againſt the direct power of the crown. We have nothing to apprehend from prerogative, but every thing from undue

due influence. Formerly it was the intereſt of the people, that the privileges of parliament ſhould be left unlimited and undefined. At preſent it is not only their intereſt, but I hold it to be eſſentially neceſſary to the preſervation of the conſtitution, that the privileges of parliament ſhould be ſtrictly aſcertained, and confined within the narroweſt bounds the nature of their inſtitution will admit of. Upon the ſame principle, on which I would have reſiſted prerogative in the laſt century, I now reſiſt privilege. It is indifferent to me, whether the crown, by its own immediate act, impoſes new, and diſpenſes with old laws, or whether the ſame arbitrary power produces the ſame effects through the medium of the houſe of commons. We truſted our repreſentatives with privileges for their own defence and ours. We cannot hinder their deſertion, but we can prevent their carrying over their arms to the ſervice of the enemy.—It will be ſaid, that I begin with endeavouring to reduce the argument concerning privilege to a mere queſtion of convenience;—that I deny at one moment what I would allow at another; and that to reſiſt the power of a proſtituted houſe of commons may eſtabliſh a precedent injurious

to

to all future parliaments.—To this I anſwer generally, that human affairs are in no inſtance governed by ſtrict poſitive right. If change of circumſtances were to have no weight in directing our conduct and opinions, the mutual intercourſe of mankind would be nothing more than a contention between poſitive and equitable right. Society would be a ſtate of war, and law itſelf would be injuſtice. On this general ground, it is highly reaſonable, that the degree of our ſubmiſſion to privileges, which have never been defined by any poſitive law, ſhould be conſidered as a queſtion of convenience, and proportioned to the confidence we repoſe in the integrity of our repreſentatives. As to the injury we may do to any future and more reſpectable houſe of commons, I own I am not now ſanguine enough to expect a more plentiful harveſt of parliamentary virtue in one year than another. Our political climate is ſeverely altered; and, without dwelling upon the depravity of modern times, I think no reaſonable man will expect that, as human nature is conſtituted, the enormous influence of the crown ſhould ceaſe to prevail over the virtue of individuals. The miſchief lies too deep to be cured by any remedy, leſs than

than ſome great convulſion, which may either carry back the conſtitution to its original principles, or utterly deſtroy it. I do not doubt that, in the firſt ſeſſion after the next election, ſome popular meaſures may be adopted. The preſent houſe of commons have injured themſelves by a too early and public profeſſion of their principles; and if a ſtrain of proſtitution, which had no example, were within the reach of emulation, it might be imprudent to hazard the experiment too ſoon. But after all, Sir, it is very immaterial whether a houſe of commons ſhall preſerve their virtue for a week, a month, or a year. The influence, which makes a ſeptennial parliament dependent upon the pleaſure of the crown, has a permanent operation, and cannot fail of ſucceſs.—My premiſes, I know, will be denied in argument, but every man's conſcience tells him they are true. It remains then to be conſidered, whether it be for the intereſt of the people that privilege of parliament (which *, in reſpect to the purpoſes, for which it has hitherto been acquieſced

* "The neceſſity of ſecuring the houſe of commons a-"gainſt the King's power, ſo that no interruption might be "given either to the attendance of the members in parlia-"ment, or to the freedom of debate, was the foundation of "parlia-

quiesced under, is merely nominal) should be contracted within some certain limits, or whether the subject shall be left at the mercy of a power, arbitrary upon the face of it, and notoriously under the direction of the crown.

I DO not mean to decline the question of *right*. On the contrary, Sir, I join issue with the advocates for privilege and affirm, that, " excepting the cases, wherein the " house of commons are a court of judicature, " [to which, from the nature of their office, " a coercive power must belong] and except- " ing such contempts as immediately interrupt " their proceedings, they have no legal au- " thority to imprison any man for any sup- " posed violation of privilege whatsoever."— It is not pretended that privilege, as now claimed, has ever been defined or confirmed by statute; neither can it be said, with any colour of truth, to be a part of the common

" parliamentary privilege; and we may observe, in all the ad- " dresses of new appointed Speakers to the Sovereign, the ut- " most privilege they demand is liberty of speech and freedom " from arrests. The very word privilege, means no more " than immunity, or a safeguard to the party who possesses " it, and can never be construed into an active power of invad- " ing the rights of others."

law of England, which had grown into prescription, long before we knew any thing of the existence of a house of commons. As for the law of parliament it is only another name for the privilege in question; and since the power of creating new privileges has been formally renounced by both houses,—since there is no code, in which we can study the law of parliament, we have but one way left to make ourselves acquainted with it;—that is, to compare the nature of the institution of a house of commons, with the facts upon record. To establish a claim of privilege in either house, and to distinguish original right from usurpation, it must appear that it is indispensably necessary for the performance of the duty they are employed in, and also that it has been uniformly allowed. From the first part of this description it follows clearly, that whatever privilege does of right belong to the present house of commons, did equally belong to the first assembly of their predecessors, was as compleatly vested in them, and might have been exercised in the same extent. From the second we must infer that privileges, which for several centuries, were not only never allowed, but never even claimed by the house of commons, must be founded

upon

upon ufurpation. The conftitutional duties of a houfe of commons, are not very complicated nor myfterious. They are to propofe or affent to wholefome laws for the benefit of the nation. They are to grant the neceffary aids to the King;—petition for the redrefs of grievances, and profecute treafon or high crimes againft the ftate. If unlimited privilege be neceffary to the performance of thefe duties, we have reafon to conclude that, for many centuries after the inftitution of the houfe of commons, they were never performed. I am not bound to prove a negative, but I appeal to the Englifh hiftory when I affirm that, with the exceptions already ftated, (which yet I might fafely relinquifh) there is no precedent, from the year 1265 to the death of Queen Elizabeth, of the houfe of commons having imprifoned any man (not a member of their houfe) for contempt or breach of privilege. In the moft flagrant cafes, and when their acknowledged privileges were moft grofsly violated, the *poor Commons*, as they then ftiled themfelves, never took the power of punifhment into their own hands. They either fought redrefs by petition to the King, or, what is more remarkable, applied for juftice to the houfe of lords;

and

and when satisfaction was denied them or delayed, their only remedy was to refuse proceeding upon the King's business. So little conception had our ancestors of the monstrous doctrines, now maintained concerning privilege, that, in the reign of Elizabeth, even liberty of speech, the vital principle of a deliberative assembly, was restrained, by the Queen's authority, to a simple *aye* or *no*, and this restriction, though imposed upon three successive parliaments*, was never once disputed by the house of commons.

I KNOW there are many precedents of arbitrary commitments for contempt. But, besides that they are of too modern a date to warrant a presumption that such a power was originally vested in the house of commons,—*Fact* alone does not constitute *Right*. If it does, general warrants were lawful.—An ordinance of the two houses has a force equal to law; and the criminal jurisdiction assumed by the Commons in 1621, in the case of Edward Loyd is a good precedent, to warrant the like proceedings against any man, who shall unadvisedly mention the folly of a King,

* In the years 1593---1597---and 1601.

 or

or the ambition of a Princeſs.—The truth is, Sir, that the greateſt and moſt exceptionable part of the privileges now contended for, were introduced and aſſerted by a houſe of commons which aboliſhed both monarchy and peerage, and whoſe proceedings, although they ended in one glorious act of ſubſtantial juſtice, could no way be reconciled to the forms of the conſtitution. Their ſucceſſors profited by the example, and confirmed their power by a moderate or a popular uſe of it. Thus it grew by degrees, from a notorious innovation at one period, to be tacitly admitted as the privilege of parliament at another.

If however it could be proved, from conſiderations of neceſſity or convenience, that an unlimited power of commitment ought to be intruſted to the houſe of commons, and that *in fact* they have exerciſed it without oppoſition, ſtill, in contemplation of law, the preſumption is ſtrongly againſt them. It is a leading maxim of the laws of England (and, without it, all laws are nugatory) that there is no right without a remedy, nor any legal power without a legal courſe to carry it into effect.

effect. Let the power, now in question, be tried by this rule. The Speaker issues his warrant of attachment. The party attached either resists force with force, or appeals to a magistrate, who declares the warrant illegal, and discharges the prisoner. Does the law provide no legal means for inforcing a legal warrant? Is there no regular proceeding pointed out in our law books to assert and vindicate the authority of so high a court as the house of commons? The question is answered directly by the fact. Their unlawful commands are resisted, and they have no remedy. The imprisonment of their own members is revenge indeed, but it is no assertion of the privilege they contend for*. Their whole proceeding stops, and there they stand, ashamed to retreat, and unable to advance. Sir, these ignorant men should be informed that the execution of the laws of Eng-

* Upon their own principles, they should have committed Mr. Wilkes, who had been guilty of a greater offence than even the Lord-Mayor or Alderman Oliver. But after repeatedly ordering him to attend, they at last adjourned beyond the day appointed for his attendance, and by this mean, pitiful evasion, gave up the point.---Such is the force of conscious guilt!

land is not left in this uncertain, defenceless condition. If the process of the courts of Westminster-hall be resisted, they have a direct course, sufficient to inforce submission. The court of King's Bench commands the Sheriff to raise the *posse comitatûs*. The courts of Chancery and Exchequer issue a *writ of rebellion*, which must also be supported, if necessary, by the power of the county.—To whom will our honest representatives direct *their* writ of rebellion? The guards, I doubt not, are willing enough to be employed, but they know nothing of the doctrine of writs, and may think it necessary to wait for a letter from Lord Barrington.

IT may now be objected to me, that my arguments prove too much; for that certainly there may be instances of contempt and insult to the house of commons, which do not fall within my own exceptions, yet, in regard to the dignity of the house, ought not to pass unpunished. Be it so.—The courts of criminal jurisdiction are open to prosecutions, which the Attorney General may commence by information or indictment. A libel, tending to asperse or vilify the house of of commons, or any of their members, may be as ſeverely puniſhed in the court of King's-bench, as a libel upon the King. Mr. De Grey thought ſo, when he drew up the information upon my letter to his Majeſty, or he had no meaning in charging it to be a ſcandalous libel upon the houſe of commons. In *my* opinion, they would conſult their real dignity much better, by appealing to the laws when they are offended, than by violating the firſt principle of natural juſtice, which forbids us to be judges, when we are parties to the cauſe*.

I DO not mean to purſue them through the remainder of their proceedings. In their firſt reſolutions, it is poſſible they might have been deceived by ill-conſidered precedents.

* "If it be demanded, in caſe a ſubject ſhould be committed by either houſe, for a matter manifeſtly out of their juriſdiction, what remedy can he have? I anſwer, that it cannot well be imagined that the law, which favours nothing more than the liberty of the ſubject, ſhould give us a remedy againſt commitments by the King himſelf, appearing to be illegal, and yet give us no manner of redreſs againſt a commitment by our fellow ſubjects, equally appearing to be unwarranted. But as this is a caſe, which I am perſuaded will never happen, it ſeems needleſs over nicely to examine it.--*Hawkins* 2. 110." ——*N. B. He was a good lawyer, but no prophet.*

For

For the reſt, there is no colour of palliation or excuſe. They have adviſed the King to reſume a power of diſpenſing with the laws by royal proclamation *; and Kings we ſee are ready enough to follow ſuch advice.—By mere violence, and without the ſhadow of right, they have expunged the record of a judicial proceeding †. Nothing remained, but to attribute to their own vote a power of ſtopping the whole diſtribution of criminal and civil juſtice.

THE public virtues of the chief magiſtrate have long ſince ceaſed to be in queſtion. But it is ſaid that he has private good qualities, and I myſelf have been ready to acknowledge them. They are now brought to the teſt.

* That their practice might be every way conformable to their principles, the houſe proceeded to adviſe the crown to publiſh a proclamation univerſally acknowledged to be illegal. Mr. Moreton publicly proteſted againſt it before it was iſſued; and Lord Mansfield, though not ſcrupulous to an extreme, ſpeaks of it with horror. It is remarkable enough that the very men, who adviſed the proclamation, and who hear it arraigned every day both within doors and without, are not daring enough to utter one word in its defence, nor have they ventured to take the leaſt notice of Mr. Wilkes for diſcharging the perſons apprehended under it.

† Lord Chatham very properly called this the act of a mob, not of a ſenate.

If he loves his people, he will diſſolve a parliament, which they can never confide in or reſpect.—If he has any regard for his own honour, he will diſdain to be any longer connected with ſuch abandoned proſtitution. But if it were conceivable, that a King of this country had loſt all ſenſe of perſonal honour, and all concern for the welfare of his ſubjects, I confeſs, Sir, I ſhould be contented to renounce the forms of the conſtitution once more, if there were no other way to obtain ſubſtantial juſtice for the people *.

JUNIUS.

* When Mr. Wilkes was to be puniſhed, they made no ſcruple about the privileges of parliament; and although it was as well known as any matter of public record and uninterrupted cuſtom could be, *that the members of either houſe are privileged except in caſe of treaſon, felony, or breach of peace,* they declared without heſitation *that privilege of parliament did not extend to the caſe of a ſeditious libel*; and undoubtedly they would have done the ſame if Mr. Wilkes had been proſecuted for any other miſdemeanor whatſoever. The miniſtry are of a ſudden grown wonderfully careful of privileges, which their predeceſſors were as ready to invade. The known laws of the land, the rights of the ſubject, the ſanctity of charters, and the reverence due to our magiſtrates, muſt all give way, without queſtion or reſiſtance, to a privilege of which no man knows either the origin or the extent. The houſe of commons judge of their own privileges without appeal:—they may take offence

offence at the moſt innocent action, and impriſon the perſon who offends them, during their arbitrary will and pleaſure, The party has no remedy;---he cannot appeal from their juriſdiction; and if he queſtions the privilege, which he is ſuppoſed to have violated, it becomes an aggravation of his offence, Surely this doctrine is not to be found in Magna Charta. If it be admitted without limitation, I affirm that there is neither law nor liberty in this kingdom. We are the ſlaves of the houſe of commons, and, through them, we are the ſlaves of the King and his miniſters. *Anonymous.*

LETTER XLV.

TO THE PRINTER OF THE PUBLIC ADVERTISER.

SIR, 1. *May*, 1771.

THEY, who object to detached parts of Junius's laſt letter, either do not mean him fairly, or have not conſidered the general ſcope and courſe of his argument, —There are degrees in all the private vices, —Why not in public proſtitution?—The influence of the crown naturally makes a ſeptennial parliament dependent.—Does it follow that every houſe of commons will plunge at once into the *loweſt depths* of proſtitution? —Junius ſuppoſes that the preſent houſe of commons, in going ſuch enormous lengths, have

have been *imprudent to themselves*, as well as wicked to the public;—that their example is *not within the reach of emulation*;—and that, in the first session after the next election, *some* popular measures may probably be adopted. He does not expect that a dissolution of parliament will destroy corruption, but that at least it will be a check and terror to their successors, who will have seen that, *in flagrant cases*, their constituents *can* and *will* interpose with effect.—After all, Sir, will you not endeavour to remove or alleviate the most dangerous symptoms, because you cannot eradicate the disease? Will you not punish *treason* or *parricide*, because the sight of a gibbet does not prevent highway robberies? When the main argument of Junius is admitted to be unanswerable, I think it would become the minor critic, who hunts for blemishes, to be a little more distrustful of his own sagacity.—The other objection is hardly worth an answer. When Junius observes that Kings are ready enough to follow *such* advice, he does not mean to insinuate that, if the advice of parliament were good, the King would be so ready to follow it.

PHILO JUNIUS.

LET-

LETTER XLVI.

ADDRESSED TO THE PRINTER OF THE PUBLIC ADVERTISER.

SIR, 22. *May*, 1771.

VERY early in the debate upon the decision of the Middlesex election, it was well observed by *Junius*, that the house of commons had not only exceeded their boasted precedent of the expulsion and subsequent incapacitation of Mr. Walpole, but that they had not even adhered to it strictly as far as it went. After convicting Mr. Dyson of giving a false quotation from the journals, and having explained the purpose, which that contemptible fraud was intended to answer, he proceeds to state the vote itself, by which Mr. Walpole's supposed incapacity was declared,—viz. "Resolved, That Robert Walpole, Esq; having been this session "of parliament committed a prisoner to the "Tower, and expelled this house for a high "breach of trust in the execution of his office, and notorious corruption when secretary at war, was and is incapable of being "elected

"elected a member to serve in this present "parliament."—And then observes that, from the terms of the vote, we have no right to annex the incapacitation to the *expulsion* only, for that, as the proposition stands, it must arise equally from the expulsion and the commitment to the Tower. I believe, Sir, no man, who knows any thing of dialectics, or who understands English, will dispute the truth and fairness of this construction. But *Junius* has a great authority to support him, which, to speak with the Duke of Grafton, I accidentally met with this morning in the course of my reading. It contains an admonition, which cannot be repeated too often. Lord Sommers, in his excellent tract upon the rights of the people, after reciting the votes of the convention, of the 28th of January, 1689, viz.—"That "King James the Second, having endea-"voured to subvert the constitution of this "kingdom by breaking the original contract "between King and people; and by the ad-"vice of jesuits and other wicked persons "having violated the fundamental laws, and "having withdrawn himself out of this king-"dom, hath abdicated the government, &c." —makes this observation upon it. "The "word *abdicated* relates to *all* the clauses "aforegoing, as well as to his deserting the "kingdom, or else they would have been "wholly in vain." And that there might be no pretence for confining the *abdication* merely to the *withdrawing*, Lord Sommers farther observes, *That King James, by refusing to govern us according to that law, by which he held the crown, did implicitly renounce his title to it.*

If *Junius's* construction of the vote against Mr. Walpole be now admitted, (and indeed I cannot comprehend how it can honestly be disputed) the advocates of the house of commons must either give up their precedent entirely, or be reduced to the necessity of maintaining one of the grossest absurdities imaginable, viz. "That a commitment to the "Tower is a constituent part of, and con- "tributes half at least to the incapacitation of "the person who suffers it."

I need not make you any excuse for endeavouring to keep alive the attention of the public to the decision of the Middlesex election. The more I consider it, the more I am convinced that, as a *fact*, it is indeed highly

highly injurious to the rights of the people; but that, as a *precedent*, it is one of the most dangerous that ever was established against those who are to come after us. Yet I am so far a moderate man, that I verily believe the majority of the house of commons, when they passed this dangerous vote, neither understood the question, nor knew the consequence of what they were doing. Their motives were rather despicable than criminal in the extreme. One effect they certainly did not foresee. They are now reduced to such a situation, that if a member of the present house of commons were to conduct himself ever so improperly, and in reality deserve to be sent back to his constituents with a mark of disgrace, they would not dare to expel him; because they know that the people, in order to try again the great question of right, or to thwart an odious house of commons, would probably overlook his immediate unworthiness, and return the same person to parliament.—But, in time, the precedent will gain strength. A future house of commons will have no such apprehensions, consequently will not scruple to follow a precedent, which they did not establish. The miser himself seldom lives to enjoy the fruit

of

of his extortion ; but his heir ſucceeds to him of courſe, and takes poſſeſſion without cenſure. No man expects him to make reſtitution, and no matter for his title, he lives quietly upon the eſtate.

PHILO JUNIUS.

LETTER XLVII.

TO THE PRINTER OF THE PUBLIC ADVERTISER.

SIR, 25. *May*, 1771.

I CONFESS my partiality to *Junius*, and feel a conſiderable pleaſure in being able to communicate any thing to the public, in ſupport of his opinions. The doctrine, laid down in his laſt letter, concerning the power of the houſe of commons to commit for contempt, is not ſo new as it appeared to many people, who, dazzled with the name of *privilege*, had never ſuffered themſelves to examine the queſtion fairly. *In the courſe of my reading this morning*, I met with the following paſſage in the journals of the houſe of commons. (Vol. 1ſt. page 603.) Upon occaſion,

casion of a jurisdiction unlawfully assumed by the house in the year 1621, Mr. Attorney-General *Noye* gave his opinion as follows. "No doubt but, in some cases, this house "may give judgment;—in matters of returns, "and concerning members of our house, or "falling out in our view in parliament; but, "for foreign matters, knoweth not how we "can judge it.—Knoweth not that we have "been used to give judgment in any case, but "those beforementioned."

Sir Edward Coke, upon the same subject, says, (page 604) "No question but this is a "house of record, and that it hath power of "judicature in some cases;—have power to "judge of returns and members of our house; "one, no member, offending out of the par-"liament, *when he came hither and justified it*, "was censured for it."

Now, Sir, if you will compare the opinion of these great sages of the law with *Junius*'s doctrine, you will find they tally exactly.—He allows the power of the house to commit their own members; (which however they may grossly abuse.) He allows their power in cases where they are acting as a court of judicature,

judicature, viz. elections, returns, &c.—and he allows it in such contempts as immediately interrupt their proceedings, or, as Mr. Noye expresses it, *falling out in their view in parliament.*

THEY, who would carry the privileges of parliament farther than *Junius*, either do not mean well to the public, or know not what they are doing. The government of England is a government of law. We betray ourselves, we contradict the spirit of our laws, and we shake the whole system of English jurisprudence, whenever we intrust a discretionary power over the life, liberty, or fortune of the subject, to any man, or set of men whatsoever, upon a presumption that it will not be abused.

PHILO JUNIUS.

LETTER XLVIII.

TO THE PRINTER OF THE PUBLIC ADVERTISER.

SIR, 28. *May*, 1771.

ANY man, who takes the trouble of perusing the journals of the house of commons, will soon be convinced, that very little, if any regard at all, ought to be paid to the resolutions of one branch of the legislature, declaratory of the law of the land, or even of what they call the law of parliament. It will appear that these resolutions have no one of the properties, by which, in this country, particularly, *law* is distinguished from mere *will* and *pleasure*; but that, on the contrary they bear every mark of a power arbitrarily assumed and capriciously applied:—That they are usually made in times of contest, and to serve some unworthy purpose of passion or party;—that the law is seldom declared until *after* the fact, by which it is supposed to be violated;—that legislation and jurisdiction are united in the same persons, and exercised at the ſame moment;—and that a court, from which there is no appeal, aſſumes an *original* juriſdiction in a criminal caſe;—in ſhort, Sir, to collect a thouſand abſurdities into one maſs, "we have a law, which cannot be "known becauſe it is *ex poſt facto*, the "party is both legiſlator and judge, and the "juriſdiction is without appeal." Well might the judges ſay, *The law of parliament is above us.*

You will not wonder, Sir, that, with theſe qualifications, the declaratory reſolutions of the houſe of commons ſhould appear to be in perpetual contradiction, not only to common ſenſe and to the laws we are acquainted with, (and which alone we can obey) but even to one another. I was led to trouble you with theſe obſervations by a paſſage, which, to ſpeak in luteſtring, I *met with this morning in the courſe of my reading*, and upon which I mean to put a queſtion to the advocates for privilege.—On the 8th of March 1704, (vide Journals, Vol. 14. p. 565.) the houſe thought proper to come to the following reſolutions.—1. "That no "commoner of England, committed by the "houſe of commons for breach of privilege

"or

"or contempt of that houſe, ought to be,
"by any writ of *Habeas Corpus*, made to ap-
"pear in any other place, or before any
"other judicature, during that ſeſſion of
"parliament, wherein ſuch perſon was ſo
"committed"

2. "THAT the Serjeant at Arms, at-
"tending this houſe do make no return of
"or yield any obedience to the ſaid writs
"of *Habeas Corpus*, and for ſuch his refuſal,
"that he have the protection of the houſe of
"commons" *.

WELBORE Ellis, What ſay you? Is this the law of parliament or is it not? I am a plain man, Sir, and cannot follow you through the phlegmatic forms of an oration.

* If there be in reality any ſuch law in England, as the *law of parliament*, which, (under the exceptions ſtated in my letter on privilege) I confeſs, after long deliberation, I very much doubt, it certainly is not conſtituted by, nor can it be collected from the reſolutions of either houſe, whether *enacting* or *declaratory*. I deſire the reader will compare the above reſolution of the year 1704, with the following of the 3d of April, 1628.---- "*Reſolved*, That the writ of Habeas "Corpus cannot be denied, but ought to be granted to *every* "man, that is committed or detained in priſon, or otherwiſe "reſtrained, by the command of the King, the Privy Coun- "cil, *or any other*, he praying the ſame."

Speak out, Grildrig,—ſay yes, or no.—If you ſay *yes*, I ſhall then inquire by what authority Mr. De Grey, the honeſt Lord Mansfield, and the Barons of the Exchequer, dared to grant a writ of *Habeas Corpus* for bringing the bodies of the Lord Mayor and Mr. Oliver before them, and why the Lieutenant of the Tower made any return to a writ, which the houſe of commons had, in a ſimilar inſtance, declared to be unlawful. —If you ſay *no*, take care you do not at once give up the cauſe, in ſupport of which you have ſo long and ſo laboriouſly tortured your underſtanding. Take care you do not confeſs that there is no teſt by which we can diſtinguiſh,—no evidence by which we can determine what is, and what is not the law of parliament. The reſolutions I have quoted ſtand upon your journals, uncontroverted and unrepealed;—they contain a declaration of the law of parliament by a court, competent to the queſtion, and whoſe deciſion, as you and Lord Mansfield ſay, muſt be law, becauſe there is no appeal from it, and they were made, not haſtily, but after long deliberation upon a conſtitutional queſtion.— What farther ſanction or ſolemnity will you annex to any reſolution of the preſent houſe

of

of commons, beyond what appears upon the face of thoſe two reſolutions, the legality of which you now deny. If you ſay that parliaments are not infallible, and that Queen Anne, in conſequence of the violent proceedings of that houſe of commons, was obliged to prorogue and diſſolve them, I ſhall agree with you very heartily, and think that the precedent ought to be followed immediately. But you, Mr. Ellis, who hold this language, are inconſiſtent with your own principles. You have hitherto maintained that the houſe of commons are the ſole judges of their own privileges, and that their declararion does, *ipſo facto*, conſtitute the law of parliament; yet now you confeſs that parliaments are fallible, and that their reſolutions may be illegal, conſequently that their reſolutions *do not* conſtitute the law of parliament. When the King was urged to diſſolve the preſent parliament, you adviſed him to tell his ſubjects, that *he was careful not to aſſume any of thoſe powers, which the conſtitution had placed in other hands*, &c. Yet Queen Anne, it ſeems, was juſtified in exerting her prerogative to ſtop a houſe of commons, whoſe proceedings, compared with thoſe of the aſſembly, of which you are a most worthy member, were the perfection of justice and reason.

In what a labyrinth of nonsense does a man involve himself who labours to maintain falsehood by argument? How much better would it become the dignity of the house of commons to speak plainly to the people, and tell us at once, *that their will must be obeyed, not because it is lawful and reasonable, but because it is their will.* Their constituents would have a better opinion of their candour, and, I promise you, not a worse opinion of their integrity.

PHILO JUNIUS.

LETTER XLIX.

TO HIS GRACE THE DUKE OF GRAFTON.

MY LORD, 22. *June*, 1771.

THE profound respect I bear to the gracious Prince, who governs this country with no less honour to himself than satisfaction to his subjects, and who restores you to your rank under his standard, will save you from a multitude of reproaches.

The attention I ſhould have paid to your failings is involuntarily attracted to the hand that rewards them; and though I am not ſo partial to the royal judgment, as to affirm, that the favour of a King can remove mountains of infamy, it ſerves to leſſen at leaſt, for undoubtedly it divides the burthen. While I remember how much is due to *his* ſacred character, I cannot, with any decent appearance of propriety, call you the meaneſt and the baſeſt fellow in the kingdom. I proteſt, my Lord, I do not think you ſo. You will have a dangerous rival, in that kind of fame to which you have hitherto ſo happily directed your ambition, as long as there is one man living, who thinks you worthy of his confidence, and fit to be truſted with any ſhare in his government. I confeſs you have great intrinſic merit; but take care you do not value it too highly. Conſider how much of it would have been loſt to the world, if the King had not graciouſly affixed his ſtamp, and given it currency among his ſubjects. If it be true that a virtuous man, ſtruggling with adverſity, be a ſcene worthy of the gods, the glorious contention, between you and the beſt of Princes, deſerves a circle, equally attentive and reſpectable. I think I already ſee other gods riſing from the earth to behold it.

But this language is too mild for the occaſion. The King is determined, that our abilities ſhall not be loſt to ſociety. The perpetration and deſcription of new crimes will find employment for us both. My Lord, if the perſons, who have been loudeſt in their profeſſions of patriotiſm, had done their duty to the public with the ſame zeal and perſeverance that I did, I will not aſſert that government would have recovered its dignity, but at leaſt our gracious Sovereign muſt have ſpared his ſubjects this laſt inſult *, which, if there be any feeling left among us, they will reſent more than even the real injuries they received from every meaſure of your Grace's adminiſtration. In vain would he have looked round him for another character ſo conſummate as yours. Lord Mansfield ſhrinks from his principles ;—his ideas of government perhaps go farther than your own, but his heart diſgraces the theory of his underſtanding.—Charles Fox is yet in bloſſom ; and as for Mr. Wedderburne, there is

* The Duke was lately appointed Lord Privy Seal.

ſomething about him, which even treachery cannot truſt. For the preſent therefore, the beſt of Princes muſt have contented himſelf with Lord Sandwich.—You would long ſince have received your final diſmiſſion and reward; and I, my Lord, who do not eſteem you the more for the high office you poſſeſs, would willingly have followed you to your retirement. There is ſurely ſomething ſingularly benevolent in the character of our Sovereign. From the moment he aſcended the throne, there is no crime, of which human nature is capable, (and I call upon the Recorder to witneſs it) that has not appeared venial in his ſight. With any other Prince, the ſhameful deſertion of him, in the midſt of that diſtreſs, which you alone had created, —in the very criſis of danger, when he fancied he ſaw the throne already ſurrounded by men of virtue and abilities, would have outweighed the memory of your former ſervices. But his Majeſty is full of juſtice, and underſtands the doctrine of compenſations. He remembers with gratitude how ſoon you had accommodated your morals to the neceſſity of his ſervice;—how chearfully you had abandoned the engagements of private friendſhip, and renounced the moſt ſolemn profeſ-

ſions

ſions to the public. The ſacrifice of Lord Chatham was not loſt upon him. Even the cowardice and perfidy of deſerting him may have done you no diſſervice in his eſteem. The inſtance was painful, but the principle might pleaſe.

You did not neglect the magiſtrate, while you flattered the *man*. The expulſion of Mr. Wilkes predetermined in the cabinet;—the power of depriving the ſubject of his birthright, attributed to a reſolution of one branch of the legiſlature;—the conſtitution impudently invaded by the houſe of commons;—the right of defending it treacherouſly renounced by the houſe of lords.—Theſe are the ſtrokes, my Lord, which, in the preſent reign, recommend to office, and conſtitute a miniſter. They would have determined your Sovereign's judgment, if they had made no impreſſion upon his heart. We need not look for any other ſpecies of merit to account for his taking the earlieſt opportunity to recall you to his councils. Yet you have other merit in abundance.—Mr. Hine,—the Duke of Portland,—and Mr. Yorke.—Breach of truſt, robbery, and murder. You would think it a compliment to your gallantry, if

I added rape to the catalogue;—but the ſtile of your amours ſecures you from reſiſtance. I know how well theſe ſeveral charges have been defended. In the firſt inſtance, the breach of truſt is ſuppoſed to have been its own reward. Mr. Bradſhaw affirms upon his honour, (and ſo may the gift of ſmiling never depart from him!) that you reſerved no part of Mr. Hine's purchaſe-money for your own uſe, but that every ſhilling of it was ſcrupulouſly paid to governor Burgoyne.—Make haſte, my Lord,—another patent, applied in time, may keep the OAKS * in the family.—If not, Birnham Wood, I fear, muſt come to the *Macaroni.*

THE Duke of Portland was in life your earlieſt friend. In defence of his property he had nothing to plead, but equity againſt Sir James Lowther, and preſcription againſt the crown. You felt for your friend; *but the law muſt take its courſe.* Poſterity will ſcarce believe that Lord Bute's ſon-in-law had barely intereſt enough at the treaſury to

* A ſuperb villa of Col. Burgoyne, about this time advertiſed for ſale.

get

get his grant compleated before the general election *.

ENOUGH has been ſaid of that deteſtable tranſaction, which ended in the death of Mr. Yorke,—I cannot ſpeak of it without horror and compaſſion. To excuſe yourſelf, you publicly impeach your accomplice, and to *his* mind perhaps the accuſation may be flattery. But in murder you are both principals. It was once a queſtion of emulation, and if the event had not diſappointed the immediate ſchemes of the cloſet, it might ſtill have been a hopeful ſubject of jeſt and merriment between you.

THIS letter, my Lord, is only a preface to my future correſpondence. The remainder of the ſummer ſhall be dedicated to your amuſement. I mean now and then to relieve the ſeverity of your morning ſtudies, and to prepare you for the buſineſs of the day. Without pretending to more than Mr. Bradſhaw's

* It will appear by a ſubſequent letter, that the Duke's precipitation, proved fatal to the grant. It looks like the hurry and confuſion of a young highwayman, who takes a few ſhillings, but leaves the purſe and watch behind him.---And yet the Duke was an old offender!

ſhaw's ſincerity, you may rely upon my attachment, as long as you are in office.

WILL your Grace forgive me, if I venture to expreſs ſome anxiety for a man, whom I know you do not love? My Lord Weymouth has cowardice to plead, and a deſertion of a later date than your own. You know the privy ſeal was intended for him; and if you conſider the dignity of the poſt he deſerted, you will hardly think it decent to quarter him on Mr. Rigby. Yet he muſt have bread, my Lord;—or rather he muſt have wine. If you deny him the cup, there will be no keeping him within the pale of the miniſtry.

JUNIUS.

LETTER L.

TO HIS GRACE THE DUKE OF GRAFTON.

MY LORD, 9. *July*, 1771.

THE influence of your Grace's fortune ſtill ſeems to preſide over the treaſury.—The genius of Mr. Bradſhaw inſpires Mr. Robinſon *. How remarkable it is, (and I ſpeak of it not as matter of reproach, but as ſomething peculiar to your character) that you have never yet formed a friendſhip, which has not been fatal to the object of it, nor adopted a cauſe, to which, one way or other, you have not done miſchief. Your attachment is infamy while it laſts, and which ever way it turns, leaves ruin and diſgrace behind it. The deluded girl, who yields to ſuch a profligate, even while he is conſtant, forfeits her reputation as well as her innocence, and finds herſelf abandoned at laſt to miſery and ſhame.—

* By an intercepted letter from the Secretary of the Treaſury it appeared, *that the friends of government were to be very active* in ſupporting the miniſterial nomination of ſheriffs.

Thus

Thus it happened with the beſt of Princes. Poor Dingley too!—I proteſt I hardly know which of them we ought moſt to lament;—The unhappy man, who ſinks under the ſenſe of his diſhonour, or him who ſurvives it. Characters, ſo finiſhed, are placed beyond the reach of panegyric. Death has fixed his ſeal upon Dingley, and you, my Lord, have ſet your mark upon the other.

THE only letter I ever addreſſed to the King was ſo unkindly received, that I believe I ſhall never preſume to trouble his Majeſty, in that way, again. But my zeal for his ſervice is ſuperior to neglect, and like Mr. Wilkes's patriotiſm, thrives by perſecution. Yet his Majeſty is much addicted to uſeful reading, and, if I am not ill-informed, has honoured the *Public Advertiſer* with particular attention. I have endeavoured therefore, and not without ſucceſs, (as perhaps you may remember) to furniſh it with ſuch intereſting and edifying intelligence, as probably would not reach him through any other channel. The ſervices you have done the nation,—your integrity in office, and ſignal fidelity to your approved good maſter, have been faithfully recorded. Nor have his

own

own virtues been intirely neglected. These letters, my Lord, are read in other countries and in other languages; and I think I may affirm without vanity, that the gracious character of the best of Princes is by this time not only perfectly known to his subjects, but tolerably well understood by the rest of Europe. In this respect alone, I have the advantage of Mr. Whitehead. His plan, I think, is too narrow. He seems to manufacture his verses for the sole use of the hero, who is supposed to be the subject of them, and, that his meaning may not be exported in foreign bottoms, sets all translation at defiance.

YOUR Grace's re-appointment to a seat in the cabinet was announced to the public by the ominous return of Lord Bute to this country. When that noxious planet approaches England, he never fails to bring plague and pestilence along with him. The King already feels the malignant effect of your influence over his councils. Your former administration made Mr. Wilkes an Alderman of London, and Representative of Middlesex. Your next appearance in office is marked with his election to the shrievalty.

In

In whatever meaſure you are concerned, you are not only diſappointed of ſucceſs, but always contrive to make the government of the beſt of Princes contemptible in his own eyes, and ridiculous to the whole world. Making all due allowance for the effect of the miniſter's declared interpoſition, Mr. Robinſon's activity, and Mr. Horne's new zeal in ſupport of adminiſtration, we ſtill want the genius of the Duke of Grafton to account for committing the whole intereſt of government in the city, to the conduct of Mr. Harley. I will not bear hard upon your faithful friend and emiſſary Mr. Touchet, for I know the difficulties of his ſituation, and that a few lottery tickets are of uſe to his œconomy. There is a proverb concerning perſons in the predicament of this gentleman, which however cannot be ſtrictly applied to him. *They commence dupes, and finiſh knaves.* Now Mr. Touchet's character is uniform. I am convinced that his ſentiments never depended upon his circumſtances, and that, in the moſt proſperous ſtate of his fortune, he was always the very man he is at preſent.—But was there no other perſon of rank and conſequence in the city, whom government could confide in, but a notorious Jacobite? Did you imagine that the whole body of the Diſſenters, that the whole Whig-intereſt of London would attend at the levy, and ſubmit to the directions of a notorious Jacobite? Was their no Whig magiſtrate in the city, to whom the ſervants of George the Third could intruſt the management of a buſineſs, ſo very intereſting to their maſter as the election of ſheriffs? Is there no room at St. James's, but for Scotchmen and Jacobites? My Lord, I do not mean to queſtion the ſincerity of Mr. Harley's attachment to his Majeſty's government. Since the commencement of the preſent reign, I have ſeen ſtill greater contradictions reconciled. The principles of theſe worthy Jacobites, are not ſo abſurd, as they have been repreſented. Their ideas of divine right are not ſo much annexed to the perſon or family, as to the political character of the Sovereign. Had there ever been an honeſt man among the *Stuarts*, his Majeſty's preſent friends would have been Whigs upon principle. But the converſion of the beſt of Princes has removed their ſcruples. They have forgiven him the ſins of his Hanoverian anceſtors, and acknowledge the hand of providence in the deſcent of the crown upon the head of a true *Stuart*.

In-

In you, my Lord, they alſo behold, with a kind of predilection, which borders upon loyalty, the natural repreſentative of that illuſtrious family. The mode of your deſcent from Charles the Second is only a bar to your pretenſions to the crown, and no way interrupts the regularity of your ſucceſſion to all the virtues of the *Stuarts*.

THE unfortunate ſucceſs of the reverend Mr. Horne's endeavours, in ſupport of the miniſterial nomination of ſheriffs, will I fear obſtruct his preferment. Permit me to recommend him to your Grace's protection. You will find him copiouſly gifted with thoſe qualities of the heart, which uſually direct you in the choice of your friendſhips. He too was Mr. Wilkes's friend, and as incapable as you are of the liberal reſentment of a gentleman. No, my Lord,—it was the ſolitary, vindictive malice of a monk, brooding over the infirmities of his friend, until he thought they quickened into public life; and feaſting with a rancorous rapture, upon the ſordid catalogue of his diſtreſſes. Now, let him go back to his cloiſter. The church is a proper retreat for him. In his principles he is already a Biſhop.

THE mention of this man has moved me from my natural moderation. Let me return to your Grace. You are the pillow, upon which I am determined to reſt all my reſentments. What idea can the beſt of Sovereigns form to himſelf of his own government?— in what repute can he conceive that he ſtands with his people, when he ſees, beyond the poſſibility of a doubt, that, whatever be the office, the ſuſpicion of his favour is fatal to the candidate, and that, when the party he wiſhes well to has the faireſt proſpect of ſucceſs, if his royal inclination ſhould unfortunately be diſcovered, it drops like an acid, and turns the election. This event, among others, may perhaps contribute to open his Majeſty's eyes to his real honour and intereſt. In ſpite of all your Grace's ingenuity, he may at laſt perceive the inconvenience of ſelecting, with ſuch a curious felicity, every villain in the nation to fill the various departments of his government. Yet I ſhould be ſorry to confine him in the choice either of his footmen or his friends.

JUNIUS.

LET-

LETTER LI.

FROM THE REVEREND MR. HORNE TO JUNIUS.

SIR, 13. *July* 1771.

FARCE, *Comedy*, and *Tragedy*,—*Wilkes*, *Foote*, and *Junius*, united at the ſame time, againſt one poor Parſon, are fearful odds. The two former are only labouring in their vocation, and may equally plead in excuſe, that their aim is a livelihood. I admit the plea for the *ſecond*; his is an honeſt calling, and my clothes were lawful game; but I cannot ſo readily approve Mr. Wilkes, or commend him for making patriotiſm a trade, and a fraudulent trade. But what ſhall I ſay to *Junius?* the grave, the ſolemn, the didactic! ridicule, indeed, has been ridiculouſly called the teſt of truth; but ſurely, to confeſs that you loſe your *natural moderation* when mention is made of the man, does not promiſe much truth or juſtice when you ſpeak of him yourſelf.

You charge me with "a new zeal in support of administration," and with "endeavours in support of the ministerial nomination of Sheriffs," The reputation which your talents have deservedly gained to the signature of *Junius*, draws from me a reply, which I disdained to give to the anonymous lies of Mr. Wilkes. You make frequent use of the word *Gentleman*; I only call myself a *Man*, and desire no other distinction: if you are either, you are bound to make good your charges, or to confess that you have done me a hasty injustice upon no authority.

I put the matter fairly to issue.—I say, that so far from any "new zeal in support of administration," I am possessed with the utmost abhorrence of their measures; and that I have ever shewn myself, and am still ready, in any rational manner, to lay down all I have—my life, in opposition to those measures. I say, that I have not, and never have had any communication or connexion of any kind, directly or indirectly, with any courtier or ministerial man, or any of their adherents: that I never have received, or solicited, or expected, or desired, or do now hope for,

for, any reward of any ſort, from any party or ſet of men in adminiſtration or oppoſition: I ſay, that I never uſed any "endeavours in "ſupport of the miniſterial nomination of "Sheriffs." That I did not ſolicit any one liveryman for his vote for any one of the candidates; nor employ any other perſon to ſolicit: and that I did not write one ſingle line or word in favour of Meſſrs. Plumbe and Kirkman, whom I underſtand to have been ſupported by the miniſtry.——

YOU are bound to refute what I here advance, or to loſe your credit for veracity: You muſt produce facts; ſurmiſe and general abuſe, in however elegant language, ought not to paſs for proofs. You have every advantage, and I have every diſadvantage: you are unknown, I give my name: all parties, both in and out of adminiſtration, have their reaſons (which I ſhall relate hereafter) for uniting in their wiſhes againſt me: and the popular prejudice is as ſtrongly in your favour, as it is violent againſt the Parſon.

SINGULAR as my preſent ſituation is, it is neither painful, nor was it unforeſeen. He is not fit for public buſineſs who does not even at his entrance prepare his mind for ſuch an event. Health, fortune, tranquility, and private connexions I have ſacrificed upon the altar of the public; and the only return I receive, becauſe I will not concur to dupe and miſlead a ſenſeleſs multitude, is barely, that they have not yet torn me in pieces. That this has been the only return, is my pride; and a ſource of more real ſatisfaction than honours or proſperity. I can practiſe before I am old, the leſſons I learned in my youth; nor ſhall I ever forget the words of my ancient Monitor,

"'Tis the laſt key-ſtone
"That makes the arch: the reſt that there
"were put,
"Are nothing till that comes to bind and
"ſhut.
"Then ſtands it a triumphal mark! then men
"Obſerve the ſtrength, the height, the why
"and when
"It was erected; and ſtill walking under,
"Meet ſome new matter to look up and
"wonder!"

I am, SIR,

Your humble Servant,

JOHN HORNE.

LET-

LETTER LII.

TO THE REVEREND MR. HORNE.

SIR, 24. *July* 1771.

I CANNOT descend to an altercation with you in the news-papers. But since I have attacked your character, and you complain of injustice, I think you have some right to an explanation. You defy me to prove, that you ever solicited a vote, or wrote a word in support of the ministerial aldermen. Sir, I did never suspect you of such gross folly. It would have been impossible for Mr. Horne to have solicited votes, and very difficult to have written for the news-papers in defence of that cause, without being detected and brought to shame. Neither do I pretend to any intelligence concerning you, or to know more of your conduct, than you yourself have thought proper to communicate to the public. It is from your own letters I conclude that you have sold yourself to the ministry: or, if that charge be too severe, and supposing it possible to be deceived by appearances ſo very ſtrongly againſt you, what are your friends to ſay in your defence? muſt they not confeſs that, to gratify your perſonal hatred of Mr. Wilkes, you ſacrificed, as far as depended upon *your* intereſt and abilities, the cauſe of the country? I can make allowance for the violence of the paſſions, and if ever I ſhould be convinced that you had no motive but to deſtroy Wilkes, I ſhall then be ready to do juſtice to your character, and to declare to the world, that I deſpiſe you ſomewhat leſs than I do at preſent.—But as a public man, I muſt for ever condemn you. You cannot but know,—nay you dare not pretend to be ignorant, that the higheſt gratification of which the moſt deteſtable   in this nation is capable, would have been the defeat of Wilkes. I know *that man* much better than any of you. Nature intended him only for a good humoured-fool. A ſyſtematical education, with long practice, has made him a conſummate hypocrite. Yet this man, to ſay nothing of his worthy miniſters, you have moſt aſſiduouſly laboured to gratify. To exclude Wilkes, it was not neceſſary you ſhould ſolicit votes for his opponents. We incline

the

the balance as effectually by lessening the weight in one scale, as by increasing it in the other.

The mode of your attack upon Wilkes (though I am far from thinking meanly of your abilities) convinces me, that you either want judgment extremely, or that you are blinded by your resentment. You ought to have foreseen, that the charges you urged against Wilkes could never do him any mischief. After all, when we expected discoveries highly interesting to the community, what a pitiful detail did it end in!—Some old cloaths—a Welsh poney—a French footman, and a hamper of claret. Indeed Mr. Horne, the public should, and *will* forgive him his claret and his footmen, and even the ambition of making his brother chamberlain of London, as long as he stands forth against a ministry and parliament, who are doing every thing they can to enslave the country, and as long as he is a thorn in the King's side. You will not suspect me of setting up *Wilkes* for a perfect character. The question to the public is, where shall we find a man, who, with purer principles, will go the lengths, and

and run the hazards that he has done? the ſeaſon calls for ſuch a man, and he ought to be ſupported. What would have been the triumph of that odious hypocrite and his minions, if *Wilkes* had been defeated! It was not *your* fault, reverend Sir, that he did not enjoy it compleatly.—But now I promiſe you, you have ſo little power to do miſchief, that I much queſtion whether the miniſtry will adhere to the promiſes they have made you. It will be in vain to ſay that I am a partizan of Mr. Wilkes, or perſonally your enemy. You will convince no man, for you do not believe it yourſelf. Yet, I confeſs, I am a little offended at the low rate, at which you ſeem to value my underſtanding. I beg, Mr. Horne, you will hereafter believe that I meaſure the integrity of men, by their conduct, not by their profeſſions. Such tales may entertain Mr. Oliver, or your grandmother, but truſt me, they are thrown away upon *Junius*.

You ſay you are a *man*. Was it generous, was it manly, repeatedly to introduce into a news-paper, the name of a young lady, with whom you muſt heretofore have lived on

terms

terms of politeneſs and good-humour?—but I have done with you. In *my* opinion, your credit is irrecoverably ruined. Mr. *Townſhend*, I think is nearly in the ſame predicament.—Poor *Oliver* has been ſhamefully duped by you. You have made him ſacrifice all the honour he got by his impriſonment.—As for Mr. *Sawbridge*, whoſe character I really reſpect, I am aſtoniſhed he does not ſee through your duplicity. Never was ſo baſe a deſign ſo poorly conducted.—This letter, you ſee, is not intended for the public, but if you think it will do you any ſervice, you are at liberty to publiſh it.

JUNIUS.

*** This letter was tranſmitted privately by the Printer to Mr. Horne, by Junius's requeſt. Mr. Horne returned it to the Printer, with directions to publiſh it.

LET-

LETTER LIII.

FROM THE REVEREND MR. HORNE TO JUNIUS.

SIR, 31. *July*, 1771.

YOU have disappointed me. When I told you that surmise and general abuse, in however elegant language, ought not to pass for proofs, I evidently hinted at the reply which I expected: but you have dropped your usual elegance, and seem willing to try what will be the effect of surmise and general abuse in very coarse language. Your answer to my letter (which I hope was cool and temperate and modest) has convinced me that my idea of a *man* is much superior to yours of a *gentleman*. Of your former letters I have always said *materiem superabat opus*: I do not think so of the present; the principles are more detestable than the expressions are mean and illiberal. I am contented that all those who adopt the one should for ever load me with the other.

I APPEAL

I APPEAL to the common-ſenſe of the public, to which I have ever directed myſelf: I believe they have it, though I am ſometimes half-inclined to ſuſpect that Mr. Wilkes has formed a truer judgment of mankind than I have. However of this I am ſure, that there is nothing elſe upon which to place a ſteady reliance. Trick, and low cunning, and addreſſing their prejudices and paſſions, may be the fitteſt means to carry a particular point; but if they have not common-ſenſe, there is no proſpect of gaining for them any real permanent good. The ſame paſſions which have been artfully uſed by an honeſt man for their advantage, may be more artfully employed by a diſhoneſt man for their deſtruction. I deſire them to apply their common-ſenſe to this letter of *Junius*, not for my ſake, but their own; it concerns them moſt nearly, for the principles it contains lead to diſgrace and ruin, and are inconſiſtent with every notion of civil ſociety.

THE charges which *Junius* has brought againſt me are made ridiculous by his own inconſiſtency and ſelf-contradiction. He charges me poſitively with "a new zeal in "ſupport

" ſupport of adminiſtration;" and with " en-
" deavours in ſupport of the miniſterial no-
" mination of Sheriffs." And he aſſigns two
inconſiſtent motives for my conduct: either
that I have "*ſold* myſelf to the miniſtry;"
or am inſtigated " by the ſolitary, vindictive
" *malice* of a monk:" either that I am influ-
enced by a ſordid deſire of *gain*; or am hurried
on by " perſonal *hatred* and blinded by *re-*
" *ſentment*." In his letter to the Duke of
Grafton he ſuppoſes me actuated by both:
in his letter to me he at firſt doubts which of
the two, whether intereſt, or revenge is my
motive: however, at laſt he determines for
the former, and again poſitively aſſerts that
" the miniſtry have made me promiſes;" yet
he produces no inſtance of corruption, nor
pretends to have any intelligence of a miniſterial connexion: he mentions no *cauſe* of
perſonal hatred to Mr. Wilkes, nor any *rea-*
ſon for my reſentment, or revenge; nor has
Mr. Wilkes himſelf ever hinted any, though
repeatedly preſſed. When *Junius* is called
upon to juſtify his accuſation, he anſwers,
" he cannot deſcend to an altercation with
" me in the news papers." *Junius*, who *exiſts*
only in the news papers, who acknowledges
" he has attacked my character" *there*, and
" thinks

"thinks I have ſome right to an *explanation*;" yet this *Junius* "cannot deſcend to an altercation in the news papers!" and becauſe he cannot deſcend to an altercation with me in the news papers, he ſends a letter of abuſe by the printer, which he finiſhes with telling me—"I am at liberty to *publiſh* it." This to be ſure is a moſt excellent method to avoid an altercation in the news papers!

THE *proofs* of his poſitive charges are as extraordinary, "He does not pretend to any "intelligence concerning me, or to know "more of my conduct than I myſelf have "thought proper to communicate to the pub-"lic." He does not ſuſpect me of ſuch groſs folly as to have ſolicited votes, or to have written anonymouſly in the news papers; becauſe it is impoſſible to do either of theſe without being detected and brought to ſhame. *Junius* ſays this! Who yet imagines that he has himſelf written two years under that ſignature, (and more under *others*) without being detected!—his warmeſt admirers will not hereafter add, without being brought to ſhame. But though he did never ſuſpect me of ſuch groſs folly as to run the *hazard* of being detected and brought to ſhame by *ano-*

nymous writing, he insists that I have been guilty of a much grosser folly of incurring the certainty of shame and detection by writings *signed* with my name! But this is a small flight for the towering *Junius*: "He "is FAR from thinking meanly of my abi-"lities," though he is "convinced that I "want judgment extremely," and can, "re-"ally respect Mr. Sawbridge's character," though he declares him * to be so poor a creature as not to "see through the basest "design conducted in the poorest manner!" And this most base design is conducted in the poorest manner, by a man whom he does not

* I beg leave to introduce Mr. Horne to the character of the *Double Dealer*. I thought they had been better acquainted.---"Another very wrong objection has been made by some, "who have not taken leisure to distinguish the characters. "The hero of the play (meaning *Mellefont*) is a gull, and "made a fool, and cheated.---Is every man a gull and a fool "that is deceived?---At that rate, I am afraid the two classes "of men will be reduced to one, and the knaves themselves "be at a loss to justify their title. But if an open, honest-"hearted man, who has an entire confidence in one, whom he "takes to be his friend, and who (to confirm him in his "opinion) in all appearance and upon several trials has been "so; if this man be deceived by the treachery of the other, "must he of necessity commence fool immediately, only be-"cause the other has proved a villain?"---YES, says parson *Horne*. No, says *Congreve*, and he, I think, is allowed to have known something of human nature.

suspect

ſuſpect of groſs folly, and of whoſe abilities he is FAR from thinking meanly!

SHOULD we aſk *Junius* to reconcile theſe contradictions, and explain this nonſenſe; the anſwer is ready; "he cannot deſcend "to an altercation in the news papers." He feels no reluctance to attack the character of any man: the throne is not too high, nor the cottage too low: his mighty malice can graſp both extremes: he hints not his accuſations as *opinion*, *conjecture*, or *inference*; but delivers them as *poſitive aſſertions:* Do the accuſed complain of injuſtice? He acknowledges they have ſome ſort of right to an *explanation*; but if they aſk for *proofs* and *facts*, he begs to be excuſed: and though he is no where elſe to be encountered—"he cannot "deſcend to an altercation in the news "papers."

AND this perhaps *Junius* may think "the *liberal reſentment of a gentleman*:" this ſkulking aſſaſſination he may call courage. In all things as in this I hope we differ:

"I thought that fortitude had been a mean
"'Twixt fear and raſhneſs; not a luſt obſcene

"Or appetite of offending; but a ſkill
"And nice diſcernment between good and ill.
"Her ends are honeſty and public good,
"And without theſe ſhe is not underſtood."

Of two things however he has condeſcended to give proof. He very properly produces a *young lady* to prove that I am not a man: and a good *old woman*, my grandmother, to prove Mr. Oliver a fool. Poor old ſoul! ſhe read her bible far otherwiſe than *Junius!* ſhe often found there that the ſins of the fathers had been viſited on the children; and therefore was cautious that herſelf and her immediate deſcendents ſhould leave no reproach on her poſterity: and they left none: how little could ſhe foreſee this reverſe of *Junius*, who viſits my political ſins upon my *grandmother!* I do not charge this to the ſcore of malice in him, it proceeded entirely from his propenſity to blunder; that whilſt he was reproaching me for introducing in the moſt harmleſs manner, the name of *one* female, he might himſelf at the ſame inſtant, introduce *two*.

I am repreſented alternately as it ſuits *Junius*'s purpoſe, under the oppoſite characters of a *gloomy Monk*, and a man of *politeneſs and good humour*. I am called "*a ſolitary Monk*," in order to confirm the notion given of me in Mr. Wilkes's anonymous paragraphs, that I *never laugh*: and the terms of *politeneſs* and *good humour* on which I am ſaid to have lived heretofore with the *young lady*, are intended to confirm other paragraphs of Mr. Wilkes, in which he is ſuppoſed to have offended me by *refuſing his daughter*. Ridiculous! Yet I cannot deny but that *Junius* has proved me *unmanly* and *ungenerous* as clearly as he has ſhewn me *corrupt* and *vindictive*: and I will tell him more; I have paid the preſent Miniſtry as many *viſits*, and *compliments* as ever I paid to the *young lady*, and ſhall all my life treat them with the *ſame politeneſs and good humour*.

BUT *Junius* "begs me to believe that he "meaſures the integrity of men by their "*conduct*, not by their *profeſſions*." Sure this *Junius* muſt imagine his readers as void of underſtanding, as he is of modeſty! Where ſhall we find the ſtandard of HIS integrity? By what are we to meaſure the *conduct* of this lurking aſſaſſin?—And he ſays this to me, whoſe conduct, wherever I could perſonally appear, has been as direct and open and public as my words; I have not, like him, concealed myſelf in my chamber to ſhoot my arrows out of the window; nor contented myſelf to view the battle from afar; but publicly mixed in the engagement, and ſhared the danger. To whom have I, like him, refuſed my name upon complaint of injury? what printer have I deſired to conceal me? in the infinite variety of buſineſs I have been concerned, where it is not ſo eaſy to be faultleſs, which of my actions can he arraign? to what danger has any man been expoſed, which I have not faced? *information*, *action*, *impriſonment*, or *death*? what labour have I refuſed? what expence have I declined? what pleaſure have I not renounced?—But *Junius*, *to whom no conduct belongs*, "meaſures the integrity of "men by their *conduct*, not by their pro-"feſſions;" himſelf all the while being nothing but *profeſſions*, and thoſe too *anonymous!* the political ignorance or wilful falſhood of this *declaimer* is extreme: his own *former* letters juſtify both my conduct and thoſe whom his *laſt* letter abuſes: for the public meaſures, which *Junius* has been all along defending, were

were ours, whom he attacks; and the uniform opposer of those measures has been Mr. Wilkes, whose bad actions and intentions he endeavours to screen.

LET *Junius* now, if he pleases, change his abuse; and quitting his loose hold of *interest* and *revenge*, accuse me of *vanity*, and call this defence *boasting*. I own I have a pride to see statues decreed, and the highest honours conferred for measures and actions which all men have approved: whilst those who counselled and caused them are execrated and insulted. The darkness in which *Junius* thinks himself shrouded, has not concealed him; nor the artifice of only *attacking under that signature* those he would pull down (whilst he *recommends by other ways* those he would have promoted) disguised from me whose partizan he is. When Lord Chatham can forgive the aukward situation in which for the sake of the public he was designedly placed by the thanks to him from the city: and when *Wilkes's name* ceases to be necessary to Lord Rockingham to keep up a clamour against the *persons* of the ministry, without obliging the different factions now in opposition to bind themselves beforehand to some certain points, and to ſtipulate ſome preciſe advantages to the public; then, and not till then, may thoſe whom he now abuſes expect the approbation of *Junius*. The approbation of the public for our faithful attention to their intereſt by endeavours for thoſe ſtipulations, which have made us as obnoxious to the factions in oppoſition as to thoſe in adminiſtration, is not perhaps to be expected till ſome years hence; when the public will look back and ſee how ſhamefully they have been deluded; and by what arts they were made to loſe the golden opportunity of preventing what they will ſurely experience,—a change of miniſters, without a *material* change of meaſures, and without any ſecurity for a tottering conſtitution.

But what cares *Junius* for the ſecurity of the conſtitution? He has now unfolded to us his diabolical principles. *As a public man he muſt ever condemn* any meaſure which may tend accidentally to *gratify* the Sovereign: and Mr. Wilkes is to be ſupported and aſſiſted in all his attempts (no matter how ridiculous and miſchievous his projects) *as long as he continues to be a thorn in*

the

the King's ſide!—The *cauſe of the country* it ſeems, in the opinion of *Junius*, is merely to vex the King; and any raſcal is to be ſupported in any roguery, provided he can only thereby plant *a thorn in the King's ſide*.—This is the very extremity of faction, and the laſt degree of political wickedneſs. Becauſe Lord Chatham has been ill-treated by the King and treacherouſly betrayed by the Duke of Grafton, the latter is to be "the pillow on which *Junius* will reſt his reſentment;" and the public are to oppoſe the meaſures of government from mere motives of perſonal enmity to the Sovereign!—Theſe are the avowed principles of the man who in the ſame letter ſays, "if ever he ſhould "be convinced that I had no motive but to "deſtroy Wilkes, he ſhall then be ready to "do juſtice to my character, and to declare "to the world that he deſpiſes me ſomewhat "leſs than he does at preſent!" Had I ever acted from perſonal affection or enmity to Mr. *Wilkes*, I ſhould juſtly be deſpiſed: But what does he deſerve whoſe avowed motive is perſonal enmity to the Sovereign; the contempt which I ſhould otherwiſe feel for the abſurdity and glaring inconſiſtency of

Junius,

Junius, is here ſwallowed up in my abhorrence of his principle. The *right divine* and *ſacredneſs* of Kings is to me a ſenſeleſs jargon. It was thought a daring expreſſion of Oliver Cromwell in the time of Charles the Firſt, that if he found himſelf placed oppoſite to the King in battle, he would diſcharge his piece into his boſom as ſoon as into any other man's. I go farther: had I lived in thoſe days, I would not have waited for chance to give me an opportunity of doing my duty; I would have ſought him through the ranks, and without the leaſt perſonal enmity, have diſcharged my piece into his boſom *rather* than into any other man's. The King, whoſe actions juſtify rebellion to his government, deſerves death from the hand of every ſubject. And ſhould ſuch a time arrive, I ſhall be as free to act as to ſay. But till then, my attachment to the perſon and family of the Sovereign ſhall ever be found more zealous and ſincere than that of his flatterers. I would offend the Sovereign with as much reluctance as the parent; but if the happineſs and ſecurity of the whole family made it neceſſary, ſo far and no farther, I would offend him without remorſe.

But let us consider a little whither these principles of *Junius* would lead us. Should Mr. Wilkes once more commission Mr. Thomas Walpole to procure for him a pension of *one thousand pounds* upon the Irish establishment for thirty years; he must be supported in the demand by the public—because it would mortify the King!

Should he wish to see Lord Rockingham and his friends once more in administration, *unclogged by any stipulations for the people*, that he might again enjoy a *pension of one thousand and forty pounds* a year, viz. From the *First Lord of the Treasury* 500 l. From the *Lords of the Treasury* 60 l. each. From the *Lords of Trade*, 40 l. each, &c. The public must give up their attention to points of national benefit, and assist Mr. Wilkes in his attempt—because it would mortify the King!

Should he demand the Government of *Canada*, or of *Jamaica*, or the embassy to *Constantinople*; and in case of refusal threaten to write them down, as he had before served another administration, in a year and a half; he must be supported in his pretensions and

upheld

upheld in his insolence—because it would mortify the King!

Junius may chuse to suppose that these things cannot happen! But that they have happened, notwithstanding Mr. Wilkes's denial, I do aver. I maintain that Mr. Wilkes did commission Mr. Thomas Walpole to solicit for him a pension of *one thousand pounds* on the *Irish* establishment for *thirty years*; with which and a pardon he declared he would be satisfied: and that, notwithstanding his letter to Mr. Onslow, he did accept a *clandestine*, *precarious* and *eleemosinary* pension from the Rockingham administration; which they paid in proportion to and out of their salaries; and so entirely was it ministerial, that as any of them went out of the ministry, their names were scratched out of the list, and they contributed no longer. I say, he did solicit the governments and the embassy, and threatened their refusal nearly in these words—"It cost me a year "and a half to write down the last admini- "stration, should I employ as much time "upon you, very few of you would be in at "the death." When these threats did not pre-

vail,

vail, he came over to England to embarraſs them by his preſence; and when he found that Lord Rockingham was ſomething firmer and more manly than he expected, and refuſed to be bullied—-into what he could not perform, Mr. Wilkes declared that he could not leave England without money; and the Duke of Portland and Lord Rockingham purchaſed his abſence with *one hundred pounds a piece*; with which he returned to Paris. And for the truth of what I here advance, I appeal to the Duke of Portland, to Lord Rockingham, to Lord John Cavendiſh, to Mr. Walpole, &c.—I appeal to the hand-writing of Mr. Wilkes, which is ſtill extant.

SHOULD Mr. Wilkes afterwards (failing in this wholeſale trade) chuſe to dole out his popularity by the pound, and expoſe the city offices to ſale to his brother, his attorney, &c. *Junius* will tell us, it is only an *ambition* that he has to make them *chamberlain*, *town-clerk*, &c. and he muſt not be oppoſed in thus robbing the ancient citizens of their birth-right—becauſe any defeat of Mr. Wilkes would gratify the King!

SHOULD

SHOULD he, after consuming the whole of his own fortune and that of his wife, and incurring a debt of *twenty thousand pounds* merely by his own private extravagance, without a single service or exertion all this time for the public, whilst his estate remained; should he, at length, being undone, commence patriot, have the good fortune to be illegally persecuted, and in consideration of that illegality be espoused by a few gentlemen of the purest public principles; should his debts, (though none of them were contracted for the public) and all his other incumbrances be discharged; should he be offered 600 l. or 1000 l. a year to make him independent for the future; and should he, after all, instead of gratitude for these services, insolently forbid his benefactors to bestow their own money upon any other object but himself, and revile them for setting any bounds to their supplies; *Junius* (who, any more than Lord Chatham, never contributed one farthing to these enormous expences) will tell them, that if they think of converting the supplies of Mr. Wilkes's private extravagance to the support of public measures——they are as great fools as my *grandmother*; and that Mr. Wilkes

Wilkes ought to hold the ſtrings of their purſes—*as long as he continues to be a thorn in the King's ſide!*

UPON theſe principles I never have acted, and I never will act. In my opinion, it is leſs diſhonourable to be the creature of a court than the tool of a faction. I will not be either. I underſtand the two great leaders of oppoſition to be Lord Rockingham and Lord Chatham; under one of whoſe banners all the oppoſing members of both houſes, who deſire to get places, enliſt. I can place no confidence in either of them, or in any others, unleſs they will now engage, whilſt they are OUT, to grant certain eſſential advantages for the ſecurity of the public when they ſhall be IN adminiſtration. Theſe points they refuſe to ſtipulate, becauſe they are fearful leſt they ſhould prevent any future overtures from the court. To force them to theſe ſtipulations has been the uniform endeavour of Mr. Sawbridge, Mr. Townſend, Mr. Oliver, &c. and THEREFORE, they are abuſed by Junius. I know no reaſon but my zeal and induſtry in the ſame cauſe that ſhould intitle me to the honour of being ranked by his abuſe with perſons of their fortune and ſtation. It is a duty

duty I owe to the memory of the late Mr. Beckford to ſay, that he had no other aim than this when he provided that ſumptuous entertainment at the Manſion-houſe for the members of both houſes in oppoſition. At that time he drew up the heads of an engagement, which he gave to me with a requeſt that I would couch it in terms ſo cautious and preciſe, as to leave no room for future quibble, and evaſion; but to oblige them either to fulfil the intent of the obligation, or to ſign their own infamy, and leave it on record; and this engagement he was determined to propoſe to them at the Manſion-houſe, that either by their refuſal they might forfeit the confidence of the public, or by the engagement lay a foundation for confidence. When they were informed of the intention, Lord Rockingham and his friends flatly refuſed any engagement; and Mr. Beckford as flatly ſwore, they ſhould then—"eat none "of his broth;" and he was determined to put off the entertainment: But Mr. Beckford was prevailed upon by —— to indulge them in the ridiculous parade of a popular proceſſion through the city, and to give them the fooliſh pleaſure of an imaginary conſequence, for the real benefit only of the cooks and purveyors.

IT

It was the ſame motive which dictated the thanks of the city to Lord Chatham; which were expreſſed to be given for his declaration in favour of *ſhort parliaments:* in order thereby to fix Lord Chatham at leaſt to that one conſtitutional remedy, without which all others can afford no ſecurity. The embaraſſment no doubt was cruel. He had his choice either to offend the Rockingham party, who declared *formally* againſt ſhort parliaments, and with the aſſiſtance of whoſe numbers in both houſes he muſt expect again to be miniſter; or to give up the confidence of the public, from whom finally all real conſequence muſt proceed. Lord Chatham choſe the latter: and I will venture to ſay, that, by his *anſwer* to thoſe thanks, he has given up the people without gaining the friendſhip or cordial aſſiſtance of the Rockingham faction; whoſe little politics are confined to the making of matches, and extending their family connexions, and who think they gain more by procuring one additional vote to their party in the houſe of commons, than by adding their languid property and feeble character to the abilities of a *Chatham*, or the confidence of a public.

WHATEVER may be the event of the present wretched ſtate of politics in this country, the principles of Junius will ſuit no form of government. They are not to be tolerated under any conſtitution. Perſonal enmity is a motive fit only for the devil. Whoever or whatever is Sovereign, demands the reſpect and ſupport of the people. The union is formed for their happineſs, which cannot be had without mutual reſpect; and he counſels maliciouſly who would perſuade either to a wanton breach of it. When it is baniſhed by either party, and when every method has been tried in vain to reſtore it, there is no remedy but a divorce: But even then he muſt have a hard and a wicked heart indeed who puniſhes the greateſt criminal merely for the ſake of the puniſhment; and who does not let fall a tear for every drop of blood that is ſhed in a public ſtruggle, however juſt the quarrel.

JOHN HORNE.

LETTER LIV.

TO THE PRINTER OF THE PUBLIC ADVERTISER.

SIR, 15. *Aug.* 1771.

I OUGHT to make an apology to the Duke of Grafton, for ſuffering any part of my attention to be diverted from his Grace to Mr. Horne. I am not juſtified by the ſimilarity of their diſpoſitions. Private vices, however deteſtable, have not dignity ſufficient to attract the cenſure of the preſs, unleſs they are united with the power of doing ſome ſignal miſchief to the community. —Mr. Horne's ſituation does not correſpond with his intentions.—In my own opinion, (which I know, will be attributed to my uſual vanity and preſumption) his letter to me does not deſerve an anſwer. But I underſtand that the public are not ſatisfied with my ſilence;—that an anſwer is expected from me, and that if I perſiſt in refuſing to plead, it will be taken for conviction. I ſhould be inconſiſtent with the principles I profefs, if I declined an appeal to the good fenfe of the people, or did not willingly fubmit myfelf to the judgment of my peers.

If any coarfe expreffions have efcaped me, I am ready to agree that they are unfit for Junius to make ufe of, but I fee no reafon to admit that they have been improperly applied.

Mr. Horne, it feems, is unable to comprehend how an extreme want of conduct and difcretion can confift with the abilities I have allowed him; nor can he conceive that a very honeft man, with a very good underftanding, may be deceived by a knave. His knowledge of human nature muft be limited indeed. Had he never mixed with the world, one would think that even his books might have taught him better. Did he hear Lord Mansfield, when he defended his doctrine concerning libels?—Or when he ftated the law in profecutions for criminal converfation?—Or when he delivered his reafons for calling the houfe of lords together to receive a copy of his charge to the jury in Woodfall's trial?—Had he been prefent upon any of thefe occafions, he would have feen how poffible it is for a man of the firft talents, to

con-

confound himſelf in abſurdities, which would diſgrace the lips of an ideot. Perhaps the example might have taught him not to value his own underſtanding ſo highly.—Lord Littleton's integrity and judgment are unqueſtionable;—yet he is known to admire that cunning Scotchman, and verily believes him an honeſt man.—I ſpeak to facts, with which all of us are converſant,—I ſpeak to men and to their experience, and will not deſcend to anſwer the little ſneering ſophiſtries of a collegian.—Diſtinguiſhed talents are not neceſſarily connected with diſcretion. If there be any thing remarkable in the character of Mr. Horne, it is that extreme want of judgment ſhould be united with his very moderate capacity. Yet I have not forgotten the acknowledgment I made him. He owes it to my bounty; and though his letter has lowered him in my opinion, I ſcorn to retract the charitable donation.

I SAID it would be *very difficult* for Mr. Horne to write directly in defence of a miniſterial meaſure, and not be detected; and even that difficulty I confined to *his* particular ſituation. He changes the terms of the propoſition, and ſuppoſes me to aſſert, that it would be *impoſſible* for *any* man to write for the news-papers and not be diſcovered.

He repeatedly affirms or intimates at leaſt, that he knows the author of theſe letters.—With what colour of truth then can he pretend *that I am no where to be encountered but in a news-paper?*—I ſhall leave him to his ſuſpicions. It is not neceſſary that I ſhould confide in the honour or diſcretion of a man, who already ſeems to hate me with as much rancour, as if I had formerly been his friend. —But he aſſerts that he has traced me thro' a variety of ſignatures. To make the diſcovery of any importance to his purpoſe, he ſhould have proved, either that the fictitious character of *Junius* has not been conſiſtently ſupported, or that the author has maintained different principles under different ſignatures.—I cannot recall to my memory the numberleſs trifles I have written;—but I rely upon the conſciouſneſs of my own integrity, and defy him to fix any colourable charge of inconſiſtency upon me.

I am not bound to aſſign the ſecret motives of his apparent hatred of Mr. Wilkes: nor does it follow that I may not judge fairly

of

of *his* conduct, though it were true *that I had no conduct of my own.*—Mr. Horne enlarges, with rapture, upon the importance of his services;—the dreadful battles which he might have been engaged in, and the dangers he has escaped.—In support of the formidable description, he quotes verses without mercy. The gentleman deals in fiction, and naturally appeals to the evidence of the poets. —Taking him at his word, he cannot but admit the superiority of Mr. Wilkes in this line of service. On one side we see nothing but imaginary distresses. On the other we see real prosecutions;—real penalties;—real imprisonment;—life repeatedly hazarded; and, at one moment, almost the certainty of death. Thanks are undoubtedly due to every man who does his duty in the engagement; but it is the wounded soldier who deserves the reward.

I DID not mean to deny that Mr. Horne had been an active partizan. It would defeat my own purpose not to allow him a degree of merit, which aggravates his guilt. The very charge *of contributing his utmost efforts to support a ministerial measure*, implies an acknowledgment of his former services.

If he had not once been diſtinguiſhed by his apparent zeal in defence of the common cauſe, he could not now be diſtinguiſhed by deſerting it.—As for myſelf, it is no longer a queſtion *whether I ſhall mix with the throng, and take a ſingle ſhare in the danger*. Whenever *Junius* appears, he muſt encounter a hoſt of enemies. But is there no honourable way to ſerve the public, without engaging in perſonal quarrels with inſignificant individuals, or ſubmitting to the drudgery of canvaſſing votes for an election? Is there no merit in dedicating my life to the information of my fellow-ſubjects?—What public queſtion have I declined, what villain have I ſpared?—Is there no labour in the compoſition of theſe letters! Mr. Horne, I fear, is partial to me, and meaſures the facility of *my* writings, by the fluency of his own.

He talks to us, in high terms, of the gallant feats he would have performed, if he had lived in the laſt century. The unhappy Charles could hardly have eſcaped him. But living princes have a claim to his attachment and reſpect. Upon theſe terms, there is no danger in being a patriot. If he means any thing more than a pompous rhapſody, let us

try,

try how well his argument holds together.— I prefume he is not yet fo much a courtier as to affirm that the conftitution has not been grofsly and daringly violated under the prefent reign. He will not fay, that the laws have not been fhamefully broken or perverted ;— that the rights of the fubject have not been invaded, or that redrefs has not been repeatedly folicited and refufed.—Grievances like thefe were the foundation of the rebellion in the laft century, and, if I underftand Mr. Horne, they would, at that period, have juftified him to his own mind, in deliberately attacking the life of his Sovereign. I fhall not afk him to what political conftitution this doctrine can be reconciled. But, at leaft, it is incumbent upon him to fhew, that the prefent King has better excufes, than Charles the Firft, for the errors of his government. He ought to demonftrate to us that the conftitution was better underftood a hundred years ago than it is at prefent ;— that the legal rights of the fubject, and the limits of the prerogative were more accurately defined, and more clearly comprehended. If propofitions like thefe cannot be fairly maintained, I do not fee how he can reconcile it to his confcience, not to act immedi-

ately

ately with the ſame freedom with which he ſpeaks. I reverence the character of Charles the Firſt as little as Mr. Horne; but I will not inſult his misfortunes, by a compariſon that would degrade him.

It is worth obſerving, by what gentle degrees, the furious, perſecuting zeal of Mr. Horne has ſoftened into moderation. Men and meaſures were yeſterday his object. What pains did he once take to bring that great ſtate criminal *Macquirk* to execution!—To-day he confines himſelf to meaſures only.—No penal example is to be left to the ſucceſſors of the Duke of Grafton.—To-morrow, I preſume both men and meaſures will be forgiven. The flaming patriot, who ſo lately ſcorched us in the meridian, ſinks temperately to the weſt, and is hardly felt as he deſcends.

I COMPREHEND the policy of endeavouring to communicate to Mr. Oliver and Mr. Sawbridge, a ſhare in the reproaches, with which he ſuppoſes me to have loaded him. My memory fails me, if I have mentioned their names with diſreſpect;—unleſs it be reproachful to acknowledge a ſincere reſpect for the character

racter of Mr. Sawbridge, and not to have questioned the innocence of Mr. Oliver's intentions.

It seems I am a partizan of the great leader of the opposition. If the charge had been a reproach, it should have been better supported. I did not intend to make a public declaration of the respect I bear Lord Chatham. I well knew what unworthy conclusions would be drawn from it. But I am called upon to deliver my opinion, and surely it is not in the little censure of Mr. Horne to deter me from doing signal justice to a man, who, I confess, has grown upon my esteem. As for the common, sordid views of avarice, or any purpose of vulgar ambition, I question whether the applause of *Junius* would be of service to Lord Chatham. *My* vote will hardly recommend him to an increase of his pension, or to a seat in the cabinet. But if his ambition be upon a level with his understanding;—if he judges of what is truly honourable for himself, with the same superior genius, which animates and directs him, to eloquence in debate, to wisdom in decision, even the pen of Junius shall contribute to reward him. Recorded honours shall gather round

round his monument, and thicken over him. It is a ſolid fabric, and will ſupport the laurels that adorn it.—I am not converſant in the language of panygeric.—Theſe praiſes are extorted from me; but they will wear well, for they have been dearly earned.

My deteſtation of the Duke of Grafton is not founded upon his treachery to any individual: though I am willing enough to ſuppoſe that, in public affairs, it would be impoſſible to deſert or betray Lord Chatham, without doing an eſſential injury to this country. My abhorrence of the Duke ariſes from an intimate knowledge of his character, and from a thorough conviction, that his baſeneſs has been the cauſe of greater miſchief to England, than even the unfortunate ambition of Lord Bute.

The ſhortening the duration of parliaments is a ſubject, on which Mr. Horne cannot enlarge too warmly; nor will I queſtion his ſincerity. If I did not profeſs the ſame ſentiments, I ſhould be ſhamefully inconſiſtent with myſelf. It is unneceſſary to bind Lord Chatham by the written formality of an engagement. He has publicly declared himſelf a cona convert to Triennial Parliaments; and tho' I have long been convinced that this is the only possible resource we have left to preserve the substantial freedom of the constitution, I do not think we have a right to determine against the integrity of Lord Rockingham or his friends. Other measures may undoubtedly be supported in argument, as better adapted to the disorder, or more likely to be obtained.

Mr. Horne is well assured, that I never was the champion of Mr. Wilkes. But tho I am not obliged to answer for the firmness of his future adherence to the principles he professes, I have no reason to presume that he will hereafter disgrace them. As for all those imaginary cases, which Mr. Horne so petulantly urges against me, I have one plain, honest answer to make to him.—Whenever Mr. Wilkes shall be convicted of soliciting a pension, an embassy, or a government, he must depart from that situation, and renounce that character, which he assumes at present, and which, in *my* opinion, intitle him to the support of the public. By the same act, and at the same moment, he will forfeit his power of mortifying the King; and though he can never be a favourite at St. James's, his base-

ness

neſs may adminiſter a ſolid ſatisfaction to the royal mind. The man, I ſpeak of, has not a heart to feel for the frailties of his fellow-creatures. It is their virtues that afflict, it is their vices that conſole him.

I GIVE every poſſible advantage to Mr. Horne, when I take the facts he refers to for granted. That they are the produce of his invention, ſeems highly probable; that they are exaggerated I have no doubt. At the worſt, what do they amount to, but that Mr. Wilkes, who never was thought of as a perfect pattern of morality, has not been at all times proof againſt the extremity of diſtreſs. How ſhameful is it, in a man who has lived in friendſhip with him, to reproach him with failings, too naturally connected with deſpair! Is no allowance to be made for baniſhment and ruin? Does a two years impriſonment make no atonement for his crimes?—The reſentment of a prieſt is implacable. No ſufferings can ſoften, no penitence can appeaſe him.—Yet he himſelf, I think, upon his own ſyſtem, has a multitude of political offences to atone for. I will not inſiſt upon the nauſeous detail, with which he ſo long diſguſted the public. He ſeems to be aſhamed of it.

But

But what excuse will he make to the friends of the constitution for labouring to promote *this consummately bad man* to a station of the highest national trust and importance? Upon what honourable motives did he recommend him to the livery of London for their representative;—to the ward of Farringdon for their alderman;—to the county of Middlesex for their knight? Will he affirm that, at that time, he was ignorant of Mr. Wilkes's solicitations to the ministry?—That he should say so, is indeed very necessary for his own justification, but where will he find credulity to believe him?

IN what school this gentleman learned his ethics I know not. His *logic* seems to have been studied under Mr. Dyson. That miserable pamphleteer, by dividing the only precedent in point, and taking as much of it as suited his purpose, had reduced his argument upon the Middlesex election to something like the shape of a syllogism. Mr. Horne has conducted himself with the same ingenuity and candour. I had affirmed that Mr. Wilkes would preserve the public favour, "as long "as he stood forth against a ministry and par- "liament, who were doing every thing they

"could

"could to enslave the country, *and* as long "as he was a thorn in the King's side." Yet, from the exulting triumph of Mr. Horne's reply, one would think that I had rested my expectation, that Mr. Wilkes would be supported by the public, upon the single condition of his mortifying the King. This may be logic at Cambridge or at the Treasury, but among men of sense and honour, it is folly or villainy in the extreme.

I SEE the pitiful advantage he has taken of a single unguarded expression, in a letter not intended for the public. Yet it is only the *expression* that is unguarded. I adhere to the true meaning of that member of the sentence, taken separately as *he* takes it, and now, upon the coolest deliberation, reassert that, for the purposes I referred to, it may be highly meritorious to the public, to wound the personal feelings of the Sovereign. It is not a general proposition, nor is it generally applied to the chief magistrate of this, or any other constitution. Mr. Horne knows as well as I do, that the best of princes is not displeased with the abuse, which he sees thrown upon his ostensible ministers. It makes them, I presume, more properly the objects of his royal compaſſion;—neither does it eſcape his ſagacity, that the lower they are degraded in the public eſteem, the more ſubmiſſively they muſt depend upon his favour for protection. This, I affirm upon the moſt ſolemn conviction, and the moſt certain knowledge, is a leading maxim in the policy of the cloſet. It is unneceſſary to purſue the argument any farther.

Mr. Horne is now a very loyal ſubject. He laments the wretched ſtate of politics in this country, and ſees, in a new light, the weakneſs and folly of the oppoſition. *Whoever or whatever is Sovereign, demands the reſpect and ſupport of the people* *, it was not ſo, *when Nero fiddled while Rome was burning.* Our gracious Sovereign has had wonderful ſucceſs, in creating new attachments *to his perſon and family.* He owes it, I preſume, to the regular ſyſtem he has purſued in the myſtery of converſion. He began with an experiment upon the Scotch, and concludes with converting Mr. Horne.—What a pity it is, that the *Jews* ſhould be condemned by Providence to wait for a Meſſiah of their own!

* The very ſoliloque of Lord Suffolk, before he paſſed the Rubicon.

The priesthood are accused of misinterpreting the scriptures. Mr. Horne has improved upon his profession. He alters the text, and creates a refutable doctrine of his own. Such artifices cannot long delude the understanding of the people; and without meaning an indecent comparison, I may venture to foretel, that the Bible and *Junius* will be read, when the commentaries of the Jesuits are forgotten.

JUNIUS.

LETTER LV.

TO THE PRINTER OF THE PUBLIC ADVERTISER.

SIR, 26. *August*, 1771.

THE enemies of the people, having now nothing better to object to my friend *Junius*, are at last obliged to quit his politics and to rail at him for crimes he is not guilty of. His vanity and impiety are now the perpetual topics of their abuse. I do not mean to lessen the force of such charges,

charges, (suppoſing they were true), but to ſhew that they are not founded. If I admitted the premiſes, I ſhould readily agree in all the conſequences drawn from them. Vanity indeed is a venial error, for it uſually carries its own puniſhment with it;—but if I thought *Junius* capable of uttering a diſreſpectful word of the religion of his country, I ſhould be the firſt to renounce and give him up to the public contempt and indignation. As a man, I am ſatisfied that he is a Chriſtian upon the moſt ſincere conviction. As a writer, he would be groſsly inconſiſtent with his political principles, if he dared to attack a religion eſtabliſhed by thoſe laws, which it ſeems to be the purpoſe of his life to defend.—Now for the proofs.—*Junius* is accuſed of an impious alluſion to the holy ſacrament, where he ſays that, *if Lord Weymouth be denied the cup, there will be no keeping him within the pale of the miniſtry.* Now, Sir, I affirm that this paſſage refers intirely to a ceremonial in the Roman catholic church, which denies the cup to the laity. It has no manner of relation to the Proteſtant creed, and is in this country, as fair an object of ridicule as *tranſubſtantiation*, or any other part of Lord *Peter*'s hiſtory in the Tale of the Tub.

But *Junius* is charged with equal vanity and impiety, in comparing his writings to the holy ſcripture.—The formal proteſt he makes againſt any ſuch compariſon, avails him nothing. It becomes neceſſary then to ſhew that the charge deſtroys itſelf.—If he be *vain*, he cannot be *impious*. A vain man does not uſually compare himſelf to an object, which it is his deſign to undervalue. On the other hand, if he be *impious*, he cannot be *vain*. For his impiety, if any, muſt conſiſt in his endeavouring to degrade the holy ſcriptures by a compariſon with his own contemptible writings. This would be folly indeed of the groſſeſt nature, but where lies the vanity?—I ſhall now be told,—"Sir, what you ſay is "plauſible enough, but ſtill you muſt allow "that it is ſhamefully impudent in *Junius* to "tell us that his works will live as long as "the Bible." My anſwer is. *Agreed: but firſt prove that he has ſaid ſo.* Look at his words, and you will find that the utmoſt he expects is, that the Bible and *Junius* will ſurvive the commentaries of the Jeſuits, which may prove true in a fortnight. The moſt malignant ſagacity cannot ſhew that his works are, *in his opinion*, to live as long as the Bible.

—Suppoſe

—Suppose I were to foretell that *Jack* and *Tom* would survive *Harry*.—Does it follow that *Jack* must live as long as *Tom*? I would only illustrate my meaning and protest against the least idea of profaneness.

YET this is the way in which *Junius* is usually answered, arraigned and convicted. These candid critics never remember any thing he says in honour of our holy religion; though it is true that one of his leading arguments is made to rest *upon the internal evidence which the purest of all religions carries with it.* I quote his words, and conclude from them, that he is a true and hearty Christian, in substance, not in ceremony; though possibly he may not agree with my Reverend Lords the Bishops, or with the Head of the Church, *that prayers are morality, or that kneeling is religion.*

PHILO JUNIUS.

LETTER LVI.

FROM THE REVEREND MR. HORNE TO JUNIUS.

17. *August*, 1771.

I CONGRATULATE you, Sir, on the recovery of your wonted ſtyle, though it has coſt you a fortnight. I compaſſionate your labour in the compoſition of your letters, and will communicate to you the ſecret of my fluency.——Truth needs no ornament; and, in my opinion, what ſhe borrows of the pencil is deformity.

YOU brought a poſitive charge againſt me of corruption. I denied the charge, and called for your proofs. You replied with abuſe and re-aſſerted your charge. I called again for proofs. You reply again with abuſe only, and drop your accuſation. In your fortnight's letter there is not one word upon the ſubject of my corruption.

I HAVE no more to ſay, but to return thanks to you for your *condeſcenſion*, and to a a *grateful* public and *honeſt* miniſtry for all the favours they have conferred upon me. The two latter, I am ſure, will never refuſe me any grace I ſhall ſolicit; and ſince you have been pleaſed to acknowledge that you told a deliberate lye in my favour out of bounty, and as a charitable donation, why may I not expect that you will hereafter (if you do not forget you ever mentioned my name with diſreſpect) make the ſame acknowledgment for what you have ſaid to my prejudice?—This ſecond recantation will perhaps be more abhorrent from your diſpoſition; but ſhould you decline it, you will only afford one more inſtance how much eaſier it is to be generous than juſt, and that men are ſometimes bountiful who are not honeſt.

At all events I am as well ſatisfied with your panegyric as Lord Chatham can be. Monument I ſhall have none; but over my grave it will be ſaid, in your own words, "*Horne's ſituation did not correſpond with his* "*intentions* *."

JOHN HORNE.

* The epitaph would not be ill ſuited to the character;--- At the beſt, it is but equivocal.

LETTER LVII.

TO HIS GRACE THE DUKE OF GRAFTON.

28. *Sept.* 1771.

MY LORD,

THE people of England are not apprifed of the full extent of their obligations to you. They have yet no adequate idea of the endlefs variety of your character. They have feen you diftinguifhed and fuccefsful in the continued violation of thofe moral and political duties, by which the little, as well as the great focieties of life, are collected and held together. Every colour, every character became you. With a rate of abilities, which Lord Weymouth very juftly looks down upon with contempt, you have done as much mifchief to the community as *Cromwell* would have done, if *Cromwell* had been a coward, and as much as *Machiavel*, if *Machiavel* had not known, that an appearance of morals and religion are ufeful in fociety.—To a thinking man, the influence of the crown will, in no view, appear fo formidable, as when he obferves to what

what enormous excesses it has safely conducted your Grace, without a ray of real understanding, without even the pretensions to common decency or principle of any kind, or a single spark of personal resolution What must be the operation of that pernicious influence, (for which our Kings have wisely exchanged the nugatory name of prerogative) that, in the highest stations, can so abundantly supply the absence of virtue, courage, and abilities, and qualify a man to be the minister of a great nation, whom a private gentleman would be ashamed and afraid to admit into his family! Like the universal passport of an ambassador, it supersedes the prohibition of the laws, banishes the staple virtues of the country, and introduces vice and folly triumphantly into all the departments of the state. Other princes, besides his Majesty, have had the means of corruption within their reach, but they have used it with moderation. In former times corruption was considered as a foreign auxiliary to government, and only called in upon extraordinary emergencies. The unfeigned piety, the sanctified religion of *George the Third* have taught him to new model the civil forces of the state. The natural resources of

the

the crown are no longer confided in. Corruption glitters in the van;—collects and maintains a ſtanding army of mercenaries, and, at the ſame moment, impoveriſhes and inſlaves the country.—His Majeſty's predeceſſors, (excepting that worthy family, from which you, my Lord, are unqueſtionably deſcended,) had ſome generous qualities in their compoſition, with vices, I confeſs, or frailties in abundance. They were kings or gentlemen, not hypocrites or prieſts. They were at the head of the church, but did not know the value of their office. They ſaid their prayers without ceremony, and had too little prieſtcraft in their underſtanding, to reconcile the ſanctimonious forms of religion with the utter deſtruction of the morality of their people.——My Lord this is fact, not declamation.—With all your partiality to the houſe *of Stuart*, you muſt confeſs, that even *Charles the Second* would have bluſhed at that open encouragement, at thoſe eager, meretricious careſſes, with which every ſpecies of private vice and public proſtitution is received at *St. James's*.—The unfortunate houſe of *Stuart* has been treated with an aſperity, which, if compariſon be a defence, ſeems to border upon injuſtice. Neither

Charles

Charles nor his brother were qualified to ſupport ſuch a ſyſtem of meaſures, as would be neceſſary, to change the government, and ſubvert the conſtitution of England. One of them was too much in earneſt in his pleaſures,—the other in his religion. But the danger to this country would ceaſe to be problematical, if the crown ſhould ever deſcend to a prince, whoſe apparent ſimplicity might throw his ſubjects off their guard,—who might be no libertine in behaviour,—who ſhould have no ſenſe of honour to reſtrain him, and who, with juſt religion enough to impoſe upon the multitude, might have no ſcruples of conſcience to interfere with his morality. With theſe honourable qualifications, and the deciſive advantage of ſituation, low craft and falſehood are all the abilities that are wanting to deſtroy the wiſdom of ages, and to deface the nobleſt monument that human policy has erected—I know *ſuch* a man;—My Lord, I know you both; and with the bleſſing of God (for I too am religious,) the people of England ſhall know you as well as I do. I am not very ſure that greater abilities would not in effect be an impediment to a deſign, which ſeems at firſt ſight to require a ſuperior capacity.

pacity. A better underſtanding might make him ſenſible of the wonderful beauty of that ſyſtem he was endeavouring to corrupt. The danger of the attempt might alarm him. The meanneſs, and intrinſic worthleſſneſs of the object (ſuppoſing he could attain it) would fill him with ſhame, repentance, and diſguſt. But theſe are ſenſations, which find no entrance into a barbarous, contracted heart. In ſome men, there is a malignant paſſion to deſtroy the works of genius, literature, and freedom. The *Vandal* and the *Monk* find equal gratification in it.

REFLECTIONS like theſe, my Lord, have a general relation to your grace, and inſeparably attend you, in whatever company or ſituation your character occurs to us. They have no immediate connexion with the following recent fact, which I lay before the public, for the honour of the beſt of Sovereigns, and for the edification of his people.

A PRINCE (whoſe piety and ſelf-denial, one would think, might ſecure him from ſuch a multitude of worldly neceſſities,) with an annual revenue of near a million ſterling, unfortunately *wants money*.—The navy of England,

land, by an equally ſtrange concurrence of unforeſeen circumſtances, (though not quite ſo unfortunately for his Majeſty) is in equal want of timber. The world knows, in what a hopeful condition you delivered the navy to your ſucceſſor, and in what a condition we found it in the moment of diſtreſs. You were determined it ſhould continue in the ſituation in which you left it. It happened, however, very luckily for the privy purſe, that one of the above wants promiſed fair to ſupply the other. Our religious, benevolent, generous Sovereign, has no objection to ſelling *his own* timber to *his own* admiralty, to repair *his own* ſhips, nor to putting the money into *his own* pocket. People of a religious turn naturally adhere to the principles of the church. Whatever they acquire falls into *mortmain*.—Upon a repreſentation from the admiralty of the extraordinary want of timber, for the indiſpenſable repairs of the navy, the ſurveyor general was directed to make a ſurvey of the timber in all the royal chaces and foreſts in England. Having obeyed his orders with accuracy and attention, he reported, that the fineſt timber he had any where met with, and the propereſt in every reſpect for the purpoſes of the navy, was in *Whittlebury*

Foreſt,

Foreſt, of which your Grace, I think, is hereditary ranger. In conſequence of this report, the uſual warrant was prepared at the treaſury, and delivered to the ſurveyor, by which he or his deputy were authoriſed to cut down any trees in *Whittlebury Foreſt*, which ſhould appear to be proper for the purpoſes above-mentioned. The deputy being informed that the warrant was ſigned and delivered to his principal in London, croſſes the country to Northamptonſhire, and with an officious zeal for the public ſervice, begins to do his duty in the foreſt. Unfortunately for him, he had not the warrant in his pocket. The overſight was enormous, and you have puniſhed him for it accordingly. You have inſiſted that an active, uſeful officer ſhould be diſmiſſed from his place. You have ruined an innocent man, and his family.—In what language ſhall I addreſs ſo black, ſo cowardly a tyrant ;—thou worſe than *one* of the *Brunſwicks*, and all the *Stuarts* !—To them, who know Lord North, it is unneceſſary to ſay, that he was mean and baſe enough to ſubmit to you.—This however is but a ſmall part of the fact. After ruining the ſurveyor's deputy, for acting without the warrant, you attacked the warrant itſelf.

You

You declared it was illegal, and ſwore, in a fit of foaming, frantic paſſion, that it never ſhould be executed. You aſſerted upon your honour, that in the grant of the rangerſhip of *Whittlebury Foreſt*, made by *Charles the Second*, (whom, with a modeſty that would do honour to Mr. Rigby, you are pleaſed to call your anceſtor) to one of his baſtards, (from whom I make no doubt of your deſcent,) the property of the timber is veſted in the ranger. —I have examined the original grant, and now, in the face of the public, contradict you directly upon the fact. The very reverſe, of what you have aſſerted upon your honour is the truth. The grant, *expreſsly, and by a particular clauſe*, reſerves the property of the timber for the uſe of the crown. —In ſpite of this evidence,—in defiance of the repreſentations of the admiralty,—in perfect mockery of the notorious diſtreſſes of the Engliſh navy, and thoſe equally preſſing, and almoſt equally notorious neceſſities of your pious Sovereign,—here the matter reſts. —The lords of the treaſury recal their warrant; the deputy-ſurveyor is ruined for doing his duty;—Mr. John Pitt, (whoſe name I ſuppoſe is offenſive to you) ſubmits to be brow-beaten and inſulted;—the oaks keep

keep their ground;—the King is defrauded, and the navy of England may perish for want of the best and finest timber in the island. And all this is submitted to—to appease the Duke of Grafton!—To gratify the man, who has involved the King and his kingdom in confusion and distress, and who, like a treacherous coward, deserted his Sovereign in the midst of it!

THERE has been a strange alteration in your doctrines, since you thought it adviseable to rob the *Duke of Portland* of his property, in order to strengthen the interest of Lord *Bute*'s son-in-law, before the last general election. *Nullum tempus occurrit regi*, was then your boasted motto, and the cry of all your hungry partizans. Now it seems a grant of *Charles the Second* to one of his bastards is to be held sacred and inviolable! It must not be questioned by the King's servants, nor submitted to any interpretation but your own.—My Lord, this was not the language you held, when it suited you to insult the memory of the glorious deliverer of England from that detested family, to which you are still more nearly allied in principle than in blood.—In the name of decency and com-

mon

mon-ſenſe, what are your grace's merits, either with King or miniſtry, that ſhould intitle you to aſſume this domineering authority over both?—Is it the fortunate conſanguinity you claim with the houſe of *Stuart?*—Is it the ſecret correſpondence you have for ſo many years carried on with Lord Bute, by the aſſiduous aſſiſtance of your *cream coloured paraſite?*—Could not your gallantry find ſufficient employment for him, in thoſe *gentle* offices by which he firſt acquired the tender friendſhip of *Lord Barrington?*—Or is it only that wonderful ſympathy of manners, which ſubſiſts between your Grace and one of your ſuperiors, and does ſo much honour to you both?—Is the union of *Blifil* and *Black George* no longer a *romance?*—From whatever origin your influence in this country ariſes, it is a phænomenon in the hiſtory of human virtue and underſtanding.—Good men can hardly believe the fact. Wiſe men are unable to account for it. Religious men find exerciſe for their faith, and make it the laſt effort of their piety, not to repine againſt providence.

JUNIUS.

LETTER LVIII.

ADDRESSED TO THE LIVERY OF LONDON.

GENTLEMEN, 30. *Sept.* 1771.

IF *you* alone were concerned in the event of the preſent election of a chief magiſtrate of the metropolis, it would be the higheſt preſumption in a ſtranger, to attempt to influence your choice, or even to offer you his opinion. But the ſituation of public affairs has annexed an extraordinary importance to your reſolutions. You cannot, in the choice of your magiſtrate, determine for *yourſelves only*. You are going to determine upon a point, in which every member of the community is intereſted. I will not ſcruple to ſay, that the very being of that law, of that right, of that conſtitution, for which we have been ſo long contending, is now at ſtake. They, who would enſnare your judgment, tell you, it is a *common*, *ordinary* caſe, and to be decided by ordinary precedent and practice. They artfully conclude, from moderate peaceable times, to times which

which *are not* moderate, and which *ought not* to be peaceable.—While they ſolicit your favour, they inſiſt upon a rule of rotation, which excludes all idea of election.

LET me be honoured with a few minutes of your attention.—The queſtion, to thoſe who mean fairly to the liberty of the people, (which we all profeſs to have in view) lies within a very narrow compaſs.—Do you mean to deſert that juſt and honourable ſyſtem of meaſures which you have hitherto purſued, in hopes of obtaining from parliament or from the crown, a full redreſs of paſt grievances, and a ſecurity for the future?—Do you think the cauſe deſperate, and will you declare, that you think ſo to the whole people of England?—If this be your meaning and opinion, you will act conſiſtently with it, in chooſing Mr. *Naſh*.—I profeſs to be unacquainted with his private character. But he has acted as a magiſtrate,—as a public man.—As ſuch I ſpeak of him,—I ſee his name in a proteſt againſt one of your remonſtrances to the crown.—He has done every thing in his power to deſtroy the freedom of popular elections in the city by publiſhing the poll upon a former occaſion; and I know, in general, that he has diſtinguiſhed himſelf, by ſlighting and thwarting all thoſe public meaſures, which *you* have engaged in with the greateſt warmth, and hitherto thought moſt worthy of your approbation.—From his paſt conduct, what concluſion will you draw, but that he will act the ſame part as *Lord Mayor*, which he has invariably acted as *Alderman* and *Sheriff?* He cannot alter his conduct, without confeſſing that he never acted upon principle of any kind.—I ſhould be ſorry to injure the character of a man, who perhaps may be honeſt in his intention, by ſuppoſing it *poſſible*, that he can ever concur with you in any political meaſure, or opinion.

IF, on the other hand, you mean to perſevere in thoſe reſolutions for the public good, which though not always ſucceſsful, are always honourable, your choice will naturally incline to thoſe men, who, (whatever they be in other reſpects,) are moſt likely to cooperate with you in the great purpoſes which you are determined not to relinquiſh:—The queſtion is not, of what metal your inſtru-

ments

ments are made, but *whether they are adapted to the work you have in hand?* The honours of the city, *in theſe times*, are improperly, becauſe excluſively, called a *reward*. You mean not merely to *pay*, but to *employ*.—Are Mr. *Croſby* and Mr. *Sawbridge* likely to execute the extraordinary, as well as the ordinary duties of Lord Mayor?—Will they grant you common halls when it ſhall be neceſſary?—Will they go up with remonſtrances to the King?—Have they firmneſs enough to meet the fury of a venal houſe of commons?—Have they fortitude enough not to ſhrink at impriſonment?—Have they ſpirit enough to hazard their lives and fortunes in a conteſt, if it ſhould be neceſſary, with a proſtituted legiſlature?—If theſe queſtions can fairly be anſwered in the affirmative, your choice is made. Forgive this paſſionate language.—I am unable to correct it.—The ſubject comes home to us all.---It is the language of my heart.

JUNIUS.

LETTER LIX.

TO THE PRINTER OF THE PUBLIC ADVERTISER.

SIR, 5. *October*, 1771.

NO man laments, more sincerely than I do, the unhappy differences, which have arisen among the friends of the people, and divided them from each other. The cause undoubtedly suffers, as well by the diminution of that strength, which union carries with it, as by the separate loss of personal reputation, which every man sustains, when his character and conduct are frequently held forth in odious or contemptible colours. ——These differences are only advantageous to the common enemy of the country.—The hearty friends of the cause are provoked and disgusted.—The lukewarm advocate avails himself of any pretence to relapse into that indolent indifference about every thing that ought to interest an Englishman, so unjustly dignified with the title of moderation.—— The false, insidious partisan, who creates or foments

foments the diſorder, ſees the fruit of his diſhoneſt induſtry ripen beyond his hopes, and rejoices in the promiſe of a banquet, only delicious to ſuch an appetite as his own.—It is time for thoſe, who really mean the *Cauſe* and the *People*, who have no view to private advantage, and who have virtue enough to prefer the general good of the community to the gratification of perſonal animoſities,—it is time for ſuch men to interpoſe.—Let us try whether theſe fatal diſſentions may not yet be reconciled; or, if that be impracticable, let us guard at leaſt againſt the worſt effects of diviſion, and endeavour to perſuade theſe furious partizans, if they will not conſent to draw together, to be ſeparately uſeful to that cauſe, which they all pretend to be attached to.—Honour and honeſty muſt not be renounced, although a thouſand modes of right and wrong were to occupy the degrees of morality between Zeno and Epicurus. The fundamental principles of Chriſtianity may ſtill be preſerved, though every zealous ſectary adheres to his own excluſive doctrine, and pious Eccleſiaſtics make it part of their religion to perſecute one another.——The civil conſtitution too, that legal liberty, that general creed, which every Engliſhman profeſſes, may ſtill be ſupported, though Wilkes, and Horne, and Townſend, and Sawbridge, ſhould obſtinately refuſe to communicate, and even if the fathers of the church, if Savil, Richmond, Camden, Rockingham, and Chatham, ſhould diſagree in the ceremonies of their political worſhip, and even in the interpretation of twenty texts in Magna Charta. —I ſpeak to the people as one of the people. —Let us employ theſe men in whatever departments their various abilities are beſt ſuited to, and as much to the advantage of the common cauſe, as their different inclinations will permit. They cannot ſerve *us*, without eſſentially ſerving themſelves.

If Mr. *Naſh* be elected, he will hardly venture, after ſo recent a mark of the perſonal eſteem of his fellow-citizens, to declare himſelf immediately a courtier. The ſpirit and activity of the Sheriffs will, I hope, be ſufficient to counteract any ſiniſter intentions of the Lord-Mayor. In colliſion with *their* virtue, perhaps he may take fire.

It is not neceſſary to exact from Mr. Wilkes the virtues of a Stoic. They were inconſiſtent

inconſiſtent with themſelves, who, almoſt at the ſame moment, repreſented him as the baſeſt of mankind, yet ſeemed to expect from him ſuch inſtances of fortitude and ſelf-denial, as would do honour to an apoſtle. It is not however flattery to ſay, that he is obſtinate, intrepid, and fertile in expedients. —That he has no poſſible reſource, but in the public favour, is, in my judgment, a conſiderable recommendation of him. I wiſh that every man, who pretended to popularity, were in the ſame predicament. I wiſh that a retreat to St. James's were not ſo eaſy and open, as Patriots have found it. To Mr. Wilkes there is no acceſs. However he may be miſled by paſſion or imprudence, I think he cannot be guilty of a deliberate treachery to the public. The favour of his country conſtitutes the ſhield, which defends him againſt a thouſand daggers. Deſertion would diſarm him.

I CAN more readily admire the liberal ſpirit and integrity, than the ſound judgment of any man, who prefers a republican form of government, in this or any other empire of equal extent, to a monarchy ſo qualified and limited as ours. I am convinced, that neither

neither is it in theory the wiseſt ſyſtem of government, nor practicable in this country. Yet, though I hope the Engliſh conſtitution will for ever preſerve its original monarchical form, I would have the manners of the people purely and ſtrictly republican.—I do not mean the licentious ſpirit of anarchy and riot —I mean a general attachment to the common weal, diſtinct from any partial attachment to perſons or families;—an implicit ſubmiſſion to the laws only, and an affection to the magiſtrate, proportioned to the integrity and wiſdom, with which he diſtributes juſtice to his people, and adminiſters their affairs. The preſent habit of our political body appears to me the very reverſe of what it ought to be. The form of the conſtitution leans rather more than enough to the popular branch; while, in effect, the manners of the people (of thoſe at leaſt who are likely to take a lead in the country) incline too generally to a dependance upon the crown. The real friends of arbitrary power combine the facts, and are not inconſiſtent with their principles, when they ſtrenuouſly ſupport the unwarrantable privileges aſſumed by the Houſe of Commons.—In theſe circumſtances, it were much to be deſired, that we had many

many ſuch men as Mr. Sawbridge to repreſent us in parliament.—I ſpeak from common report and opinion only, when I impute to him a ſpeculative predilection in favour of a republic.—In the perſonal conduct and manners of the man, I cannot be miſtaken. He has ſhewn himſelf poſſeſſed of that republican firmneſs, which the times require, and by which an Engliſh gentleman may be as uſeful, and as honourably diſtinguiſhed, as any citizen of ancient Rome, of Athens, or Lacedæmon.

Mr. Townſend complains, that the public gratitude has not been anſwerable to his deſerts.—It is not difficult to trace the artifices, which have ſuggeſted to him a language, ſo unworthy of his underſtanding. A great man commands the affections of the people. A prudent man does not complain when he has loſt them. Yet they are far from being loſt to Mr. Townſend. He has treated our opinion a little too cavalierly. A young man is apt to rely too confidently upon himſelf, to be as attentive to his miſtreſs, as a polite and paſſionate lover ought to be. Perhaps he found her at firſt too eaſy a conqueſt.—

Yet

Yet, I fancy, ſhe will be ready to receive him, whenever he thinks proper to renew his addreſſes. With all his youth, his ſpirit, and his appearance, it would be indecent in the lady to ſolicit his return.

I HAVE too much reſpect for the abilities of Mr. Horne, to flatter myſelf that theſe gentlemen will ever be cordially re-united. It is not, however, unreaſonable to expect, that each of them ſhould act his ſeparate part, with honour and integrity to the public.—As for differences of opinion upon ſpeculative queſtions, if we wait until *they* are reconciled, the action of human affairs muſt be ſuſpended for ever. But neither are we to look for perfection in any one man, nor for agreement among many.——When *Lord Chatham* affirms, that the authority of the Britiſh legiſlature is not ſupreme over the colonies, in the ſame ſenſe in which it is ſupreme over Great Britain;——when *Lord Camden* ſuppoſes a neceſſity, (which the King is to judge of) and, founded upon that neceſſity, attributes to the crown a legal power (not given by the act itſelf) to ſuſpend the operation of an act of the legiſlature,—I liſten to them both with diffidence and reſpect, but

but without the ſmalleſt degree of conviction or aſſent. Yet, I doubt not, they delivered their real ſentiments, nor ought they to be haſtily condemned.—*I too* have a claim to the candid interpretation of my country, when I acknowledge an involuntary, compulſive aſſent to one very unpopular opinion. I lament the unhappy neceſſity, whenever it ariſes, of providing for the ſafety of the ſtate, by a temporary invaſion of the perſonal liberty of the ſubject. Would to God it were practicable to reconcile theſe important objects, in every poſſible ſituation of public affairs! —I regard the legal liberty of the meaneſt man in Britain, as much as my own, and would defend it with the ſame zeal. I know we muſt ſtand or fall together. But I never can doubt, that the community has a right to command, as well as to purchaſe, the ſervice of its members. I ſee that right founded originally upon a neceſſity, which ſuperſedes all argument. I ſee it eſtabliſhed by uſage immemorial, and admitted by more than a tacit aſſent of the legiſlature. I conclude there is no remedy, in the nature of things, for the grievance complained of; for, if there were, it muſt long ſince have been redreſſed. Though numberleſs opportunities

tunities have presented themselves, highly favourable to public liberty, no successful attempt has ever been made for the relief of the subject in this article. Yet it has been felt and complained of, ever since England had a navy.—The conditions, which constitute this right, must be taken together. Separately, they have little weight. It is not fair to argue, from any abuse in the execution, to the illegality of the power; much less is a conclusion to be drawn from the navy to the land service. A seaman can never be employed but against the enemies of his country. The only case in which the King can have a right to arm his subjects in general, is that of a foreign force being actually landed upon our coast. Whenever that case happens, no true Englishman will enquire, whether the King's right to compel him to defend his country be the custom of England, or a grant of the legislature. With regard to the press for seamen, it does not follow that the symptoms may not be softened, although the distemper cannot be cured. Let bounties be increased as far as the public purse can support them. Still they have a limit; and when every reasonable expence is incurred, it will be found, in fact, that the spur of the press is wanted to give operation to the bounty.

UPON

UPON the whole, I never had a doubt about the ſtrict right of preſſing, until I heard that Lord Mansfield had applauded Lord Chatham for delivering ſomething like this doct ine in the houſe of lords. That conſideration ſtaggered me not a little. But, upon reflection, his conduct accounts naturally for itſelf. He knew the doctrine was unpopular, and was eager to fix it upon the man, who is the firſt object of his fear and deteſtation. The cunning Scotchman never ſpeaks truth without a fraudulent deſign. In council, he generally affects to take a moderate part. Beſides his natural timidity, it makes part of his political plan, never to be known to recommend violent meaſures. When the guards are called forth to murder their fellow-ſubjects, it is not by the oſtenſible advice of Lord Mansfield. That odious office, his prudence tells him, is better left to ſuch men as Gower and Weymouth, as Barrington and Grafton. Lord Hillſborough wiſely confines *his* firmneſs to the diſtant Americans.—The deſigns of Mansfield are more ſubtle, more effectual, and ſecure. —Who attacks the liberty of the preſs?—Lord Mansfield.—Who invades the conſtitutional power of juries?—Lord Mansfield.—

What

What judge ever challenged a juryman, but Lord Mansfield?—Who was that judge, who, to save the King's brother, affirmed that a man of the first rank and quality, who obtains a verdict in a suit for criminal conversation, is entitled to no greater damages than the meanest mechanic?—Lord Mansfield.—Who is it makes commissioners of the great seal?—Lord Mansfield.—Who is it forms a decree for those commissioners, deciding against Lord Chatham, and afterwards (finding himself opposed by the judges) declares in parliament, that he never had a doubt that the law was in direct opposition to that decree?—Lord Mansfield.—Who is he, that has made it the study and practice of his life, to undermine and alter the whole system of jursprudence in the court of King's Bench?—Lord Mansfield. There never existed a man but himself, who answered exactly to so complicated a description. Compared to these enormities, his original attachment to the Pretender, (to whom his dearest brother was confidential secretary) is a virtue of the first magnitude. But the hour of impeachment *will* com , and neither he nor Grafton shall escape me. Now let them make common cause against England and the house of Hanover. A Stuart and a Murray should sympathise with each other.

WHEN

WHEN I refer to ſignal inſtances of unpopular opinions delivered and maintained by men, who may well be ſuppoſed to have no view but the public good, I do not mean to renew the diſcuſſion of ſuch opinions. I ſhould be ſorry to revive the dormant queſtions of *Stamp-act*, *Corn-bill*, or *Preſs-warrant*. I mean only to illuſtrate one uſeful propoſition, which it is the intention of this paper to inculcate;—*That we ſhould not generally reject the friendſhip or ſervices of any man, becauſe he differs from us in a particular opinion.* This will not appear a ſuperfluous caution, if we obſerve the ordinary conduct of mankind. In public affairs, there is the leaſt chance of a perfect concurrence of ſentiment, or inclination. Yet every man is able to contribute ſomething to the common ſtock, and no man's contribution ſhould be rejected. If individuals have no virtues, their vices may be of uſe to us. I care not with what principle the new-born patriot is animated, if the meaſures he ſupports are beneficial to the community. The nation is intereſted in his conduct. His motives are his own. The properties of a patriot are periſhable in the individual, but there is a quick ſucceſſion of ſubjects, and the breed is worth preſerving.

 —The

—The ſpirit of the Americans may be an uſeful example to us. Our dogs and horſes are only Engliſh upon Engliſh ground; but patriotiſm, it ſeems, may be improved by tranſplanting.—I will not reject a bill, which tends to confine parliamentary privilege within reaſonable bounds, though it ſhould be ſtolen from the houſe of Cavendiſh, and introduced by Mr. Onſlow. The features of the infant are a proof of the deſcent, and vindicate the noble birth from the baſeneſs of the adoption.—I willingly accept of a ſarcaſm from *Colonel Barrè*, or a ſimile from *Mr. Burke*. Even the ſilent vote of *Mr. Calcraft* is worth reckoning in a diviſion.—What though he riots in the plunder of the army, and has only determined to be a patriot, when he could not be a peer?—Let us profit by the aſſiſtance of ſuch men, while they are with us, and place them, if it be poſſible, in the poſt of danger, to prevent deſertion. The wary *Wedderburne*, the pompous *Suffolk* never threw away the ſcabbard, nor ever went upon a forlorn hope. They always treated the King's ſervants as men, with whom, ſome time or other, they might poſſibly be in friendſhip.—When a man who ſtands forth for the public, has gone that length, from which there is no practicable retreat,—when he has given that kind of perſonal

ſonal offence, which a pious monarch never pardons, I then begin to think him in earneſt, and that he never will have occaſion to ſolicit the forgiveneſs of his country.—But inſtances of a determination ſo entire and unreſerved are rarely met with. Let us take mankind, *as they are*. Let us diſtribute the virtues and abilities of individuals, according to the offices they affect, and when they quit the ſervice, let us endeavour to ſupply their places with better men than we have loſt. In this country, there are always candidates enough for popular favour. The temple of *fame* is the ſhorteſt paſſage to riches and preferment.

ABOVE all things, let me guard my countrymen againſt the meanneſs and folly of accepting of a trifling or moderate compenſation for extraordinary and eſſential injuries. Our enemies treat us, as the cunning trader does the unſkilful Indian. They magnify their generoſity, when they give us baubles, of little proportionate value, for ivory and gold. The ſame houſe of commons, who robbed the conſtituent body of their right of free election, who preſumed to *make* a law under pretence of *declaring* it, who paid our good King's debts, without once enquiring how they were incurred; who gave thanks for repeated murders committed at home, and for national infamy incurred abroad; who ſcreened *Lord Mansfield*; who impriſoned the magiſtrates of the metropolis, for aſſerting the ſubjects right to the protection of the laws; who eraſed a judicial record, and ordered all proceedings in a criminal ſuit to be ſuſpended; —this very houſe of commons have graciouſly conſented, that their own members may be compelled to pay their debts, and that conteſted elections ſhall for the future be determined with ſome decent regard to the merits of the caſe. The event of the ſuit is of no conſequence to the crown. While parliaments are ſeptennial, the purchaſe of the ſitting member or of the petitioner makes but the difference of a day.—Conceſſions, ſuch as theſe, are of little moment to the ſum of things; unleſs it be to prove, that the worſt of men are ſenſible of the injuries they have done us, and perhaps to demonſtrate to us the imminent danger of our ſituation. In the ſhipwreck of the ſtate, trifles float and are preſerved; while every thing ſolid and valuable ſinks to the bottom, and is loſt for ever.

JUNIUS.

LETTER LX.

TO THE PRINTER OF THE PUBLIC ADVERTISER.

SIR, 15. *October*, 1771.

I AM convinced that *Junius* is incapable of wilfully misrepresenting any man's opinion, and that his inclination leads him to treat *Lord Camden* with particular candour and respect. The doctrine attributed to him by *Junius*, as far as it goes, corresponds with that stated by your correspondent *Scævola*, who seems to make a distinction without a difference. *Lord Camden*, it is agreed, did certainly maintain that, in the recess of parliament, the King, (by which we all mean the *King in council*, or the executive power) might suspend the operation of an act of the legislature; and he founded his doctrine upon a supposed necessity, of which the King, *in the first instance*, must be judge. The lords and commons cannot be judges of it in the first instance, for they do not exist.—Thus far *Junius*.

But, says *Scævola*, *Lord Camden* made *parliament*, and not the *King*, judges of the neceſſity.—That parliament may review the acts of miniſters is unqueſtionable; but there is a wide difference between ſaying that the crown has a *legal* power, and, that miniſters may act *at their peril*. When we ſay an act is *illegal*, we mean that it is forbidden by a joint reſolution of the three eſtates. How a ſubſequent reſolution of two of thoſe branches can make it *legal ab initio*, will require explanation. If it could, the conſequence would be truly dreadful, eſpecially in theſe times. There is no act of arbitrary power, which the King might not attribute to *neceſſity*, and for which he would not be ſecure of obtaining the approbation of his proſtituted lords and commons. If Lord *Camden* admits that the ſubſequent ſanction of parliament was neceſſary to make the proclamation *legal*, why did he ſo obſtinately oppoſe the bill, which was ſoon after brought in, for indemnifying all thoſe perſons, who had acted under it?—If that bill had not been paſſed, I am ready to maintain, in direct contradiction to Lord Camden's doctrine,

(taken

(taken as *Scævola* ſtates it) that a litigious exporter of corn, who had ſuffered in his property in conſequence of the proclamation, might have laid his action againſt the cuſtom-houſe officers, and would infallibly have recovered damages. No jury could refuſe them; and if I, who am by no means litigious, had been ſo injured, I would aſſuredly have inſtituted a ſuit in Weſtminſter-hall, on purpoſe to try the queſtion of right. I would have done it upon a principle of defiance of the pretended power of either or both houſes to make declarations inconſiſtent with law, and I have no doubt, that, with an act of parliament of my ſide, I ſhould have been too ſtrong for them all. This is the way, in which an Engliſhman ſhould ſpeak and act, and not ſuffer dangerous precedents to be eſtabliſhed, becauſe the circumſtances are favourable or palliating.

WITH regard to Lord *Camden*, the truth is, that he inadvertently over-ſhot himſelf, as appears plainly by that unguarded mention of *a tyranny of forty days*, which I myſelf heard. Inſtead of aſſerting that the proclamation was *legal*, he *ſhould* have ſaid, "My

 lords,

" lords, I know the proclamation was *illegal*,
" but I advised it because it was indispen-
" sably necessary to save the kingdom from
" famine, and I submit myself to the justice
" and mercy of my country."

SUCH language as this would have been manly, rational, and consistent :—not unfit for a lawyer, and every way worthy of a great man.

PHILO JUNIUS.

P. S. IF *Scævola* should think proper to write again upon this subject, I beg of him to give me a *direct* answer, that is, a plain affirmative or negative, to the following questions :—In the interval between the publishing such a proclamation (or order of council) as that in question, and it's receiving the sanction of the two houses, of what nature is it—is it *legal* or *illegal*; or is it neither one nor the other?—I mean to be candid, and will point out to him the consequence of his answer either way.—If it be *legal*, it wants no farther sanction. If it be *illegal*, the subject is not bound to obey it, consequently it is a useless, nugatory act, even as to it's declared purpose. Before the meet-

meeting of parliament, the whole mischief, which it means to prevent, will have been compleated.

LETTER LXI.

TO ZENO.

SIR, 17. *Oct.* 1771.

THE sophistry of your letter in defence of *Lord Mansfield* is adapted to the character you defend. But *Lord Mansfield* is a man of *form*, and seldom in his behaviour transgresses the rules of decorum. I shall imitate his lordship's good manners, and leave *you* in the full possession of his principles. I will not call you *liar*, *jesuit*, or *villain*; but, with all the politeness imaginable, perhaps I may prove you so.

LIKE other fair pleaders in *Lord Mansfield*'s school of justice, you answer *Junius* by misquoting his words, and mistating his propositions. If I am candid enough to admit that this is the very logic taught at *St. Omer*'s, you will readily allow that it is the constant practice in the court of *King's Bench*.

—JU-

—JUNIUS *does not ſay*, that he never had a doubt about the ſtrict right of preſſing, *till he knew Lord Mansfield was of the ſame opinion.* His words are, *until he heard that Lord Manſfield had applauded Lord Chatham for maintaining that doctrine in the houſe of lords.* It was not the accidental concurrence of Lord Mansfield's opinion, but the ſuſpicious applauſe given by a cunning Scotchman to the man he deteſts, that raiſed and juſtified a doubt in the mind of *Junius*. The queſtion is not, whether Lord Mansfield be a man of learning and abilities (which *Junius* has never diſputed,) but whether or no he abuſes and miſapplies his talents.

Junius did *not* ſay that Lord Mansfield had adviſed the calling out the guards. On the contrary, his plain meaning is, that he left that odious office to men leſs cunning than himſelf.—Whether Lord Mansfield's doctrine concerning libels be or be not an attack upon the liberty of the preſs, is a queſtion, which the public in general are very well able to determine. I ſhall not enter into it at preſent. Nor do I think it neceſſary to ſay much to a man, who had the daring confidence to ſay

to

to a jury, "Gentlemen, you are to bring in "a verdict *guilty* or *not guilty*, but whether "the defendant be guilty or innocent is not "matter for *your* consideration." Cloath it in what language you will, this is the sum total of Lord Mansfield doctrine. If not, let *Zeno* shew us the difference.

BUT it seems, *the liberty of the press may be abused*, and *the abuse of a valuable privilege is the certain means to lose it*. The *first* I admit,—but let the *abuse* be submitted to a jury, a sufficient and indeed the only legal and constitutional check upon the licence of the press. The *second*, I flatly deny. In direct contradiction to *Lord Mansfield* I affirm that "the abuse of a valuable privilege "*is not* the *certain* means to lose it." If it were, the English nation would have few privileges left, for where is the privilege that has not, at one time or other, been abused by individuals. But it is false in reason and equity, that particular abuses should produce a general forfeiture. Shall the community be deprived of the protection of the laws because there are robbers and murderers?— Shall the community be punished, because individuals have offended. Lord Mansfield says so, consistently enough with his principles,

ciples, but I wonder to find him ſo explicit. Yet, for one conceſſion, however extorted, I confeſs myſelf obliged to him.—The liberty of the preſs is after all a *valuable privilege* I agree with him moſt heartily, and will defend it againſt him.

You aſk me, What *juryman* was challenged by Lord Mansfield?—I tell you, his name was *Benſon*. When his name was called, Lord Mansfield ordered the clerk to paſs him by. As for his reaſons, you may aſk himſelf, for he aſſigned none. But I can tell you what all men thought of it. This *Benſon* had been refractory upon a former jury, and would not accept of the law as delivered by Lord Mansfield; but had the impudence to pretend to think for himſelf.—But you it ſeems, honeſt *Zeno*, know nothing of the matter! You never read *Junius*'s letter to your patron! You never heard of the intended inſtructions from the city to impeach Lord Mansfield!—You never heard by what dexterity of *Mr. Paterſon* that meaſure was prevented! How wonderfully ill ſome people are informed!

Junius did *never* affirm that the crime, of ſeducing the wife of a mechanic or a peer, is

not

not the ſame, taken in a moral or religious view. What he affirmed in contradiction to the levelling principle ſo lately adopted by Lord Mansfield was, *that the damages ſhould be proportioned to the rank and fortune of the parties*; and for this plain reaſon; (admitted by every other judge that ever ſat in Weſtminſter Hall) becauſe, what is a compenſation or penalty to one man is none to another. The ſophiſtical diſtinction you attempt to draw between the perſon *injured*, and the perſon *injuring* is *Mansfield* all over. If you can once eſtabliſh the propoſition that the injured party is not intitled to *receive* large damages, it follows pretty plainly that the party *injuring* ſhould not be compelled to *pay* them; conſequently the King's brother is effectually ſcreened by *Lord Mansfield*'s doctrine. Your reference to *Nathan* and *David* come naturally in aid of your patron's profeſſed ſyſtem of juriſprudence. He is fond of introducing into the *court of King's Bench* any law that contradicts or excludes the common law of England; whether it be *canon*, *civil*, *jus gentium*, or *levitical*. But, Sir, the Bible is the code of our religious faith, not of our municipal juriſprudence; and though it was the pleaſure of God to inflict a particular puniſh-

punishment upon David's crime (taken as a breach of his divine commands) and to send his prophet to denounce it, an English jury have nothing to do either with David or the prophet. They consider the crime, only as it is a breach of order, an injury to an individual, and an offence to society, and they judge of it by certain positive rules of law, or by the practice of their ancestors. Upon the whole, the man, *after God's own heart* is much indebted to you for comparing him to the Duke of Cumberland. That his Royal Highness may be the man after *Lord Mansfield's* own heart seems much more probable, and you I think *Mr. Zeno*, might succeed tolerably well in the character of *Nathan*. The evil deity, the prophet, and the royal sinner would be very proper company for one another.

You say Lord Mansfield did not *make* the commissioners of the Great Seal, and that he only advised the King to appoint. I believe *Junius* meant no more, and the distinction is hardly worth disputing.—

You say he *did not* deliver an opinion upon Lord Chatham's appeal.—I affirm that he *did*,

did, directly in favour of the appeal. This is a point of fact, to be determined by evidence only. But you assign no reason for his supposed silence, nor for his desiring a conference with the judges the day before. Was not all Westminster-hall convinced that he did it with a view to puzzle them with some perplexing question, and in hopes of bringing some of them over to him?—You say the commissioners were *very capable of framing a decree for themselves.* By the fact, it only appears, that they were capable of framing an *illegal* one, which, I apprehend, is not much to the credit either of their learning or integrity.

WE are both agreed that *Lord Mansfield* has incessantly laboured to introduce new modes of proceeding in the court where he presides; but *you* attribute it to an honest zeal in behalf of innocence oppressed by quibble and chicane. I say that he has introduced *new law* too, and removed the landmarks established by former decisions. I say that his view is to change a court of common law into a court of equity, and to bring every thing within the *arbitrium* of a *prætorian* court. The public must determine between us.

us. *But now for his merits. First* then, the eſtabliſhment of the judges in their places for life, (which you tell us was adviſed by Lord Mansfield) was a conceſſion merely to catch the people. It bore the appearance of a royal bounty, but had nothing real in it. The judges were already for life, excepting in the caſe of a *demiſe.* Your boaſted bill only provides that it ſhall not be in the power of the King's ſucceſſor to remove them. At the beſt therefore, it is only a legacy, not a gift on the part of his preſent Majeſty, ſince for himſelf, he gives up nothing.—That he did oppoſe *Lord Camden* and *Lord Northington* upon the proclamation againſt the exportation of corn, is moſt true, and with great ability. With his talents, and taking the right ſide of ſo clear a queſtion, it was impoſſible to ſpeak ill.—His motives are not ſo eaſily penetrated. They, who are acquainted with the ſtate of politics, at that period, will judge of them ſomewhat differently from *Zeno.* Of the popular bills, which you ſay he ſupported in the houſe of lords, the moſt material is unqueſtionably that of *Mr. Grenville*, for deciding conteſted elections. But I ſhould be glad to know upon what poſſible pretence any

any member of the upper houſe could oppoſe ſuch a bill, after it had paſſed the *houſe of commons?*—I do not pretend to know what ſhare he had in promoting the other two bills, but I am ready to give him all the credit you deſire. Still you will find that a whole life of deliberate iniquity is ill atoned for by doing now and then a laudable action upon a mixed or doubtful principle.—If it be unworthy of him, thus ungratefully treated, to labour any longer for the public, in God's name let him retire. His brother's patron, (whoſe health he once was anxious for) is dead, but the ſon of that unfortunate prince ſurvives, and, I dare ſay, will be ready to receive him.

PHILO JUNIUS.

LETTER LXII.

TO AN ADVOCATE IN THE CAUSE OF THE PEOPLE.

SIR, 18. *October*, 1771.

YOU do not treat *Junius* fairly. You would not have condemned him ſo haſtily, if you had ever read *Judge Foſter's* argument upon the legality of preſſing ſeamen. A man who has not read that argument, is not qualified to ſpeak accurately upon the ſubject. In anſwer to ſtrong facts and fair reaſoning, you produce nothing but a vague compariſon between two things, which have little or no reſemblance to each other. *General Warrants*, it is true, had been often iſſued, but they had never been regularly queſtioned or reſiſted, until the caſe of *Mr. Wilkes*. He brought them to trial, and the moment they were tried, they were declared *illegal*. This is not the caſe of *Preſs Warrants*. They have been complained of, queſtioned, and reſiſted in a thouſand inſtances; but ſtill the legiſlature have never interpoſed, nor has there

there ever been a formal decision against them in any of the superior courts. On the contrary, they have been frequently recognized and admitted by parliament, and there are judicial opinions given in their favour, by judges of the first character. Under the various circumstances, stated by *Junius*, he has a right to conclude, *for himself*, that there is no remedy. If you have a good one to propose, you may depend upon the assistance and applause of *Junius*. The magistrate, who guards the liberty of the individual, deserves to be commended. But let him remember that it is also his duty to provide for, or at least not to hazard the safety of the community. If, in the case of a foreign war and the expectation of an invasion, you would rather keep your fleet in harbour, than man it by pressing seamen, who refuse the bounty, I have done.

You talk of disbanding the army with wonderful ease and indifference. If a wiser man held such language, I should be apt to suspect his sincerity.

As for keeping up a *much greater* number of seamen in time of peace, it is not to be done. You will oppreſs the merchant, you will diſtreſs trade, and deſtroy the nurſery of your ſeamen. He muſt be a miſerable ſtateſman, who voluntarily, by the ſame act increaſes the public expence, and leſſens the means of ſupporting it.

PHILO JUNIUS.

LETTER LXIII.

22. *October*, 1771.

A FRIEND of *Junius* deſires it may be obſerved, (in anſwer to *A Barriſter at Law*)

1°. THAT the fact of Lord Mansfield's having ordered a juryman to be paſſed by (which poor *Zeno* never heard of) is now formally admitted. When *Mr. Benſon*'s name was called, *Lord Mansfield* was obſerved to fluſh in the face, (a ſignal of guilt not uncommon with him) and cried out, *Paſs him by*. This I take to be ſomething more than a peremptory challenge. It is an *unlawful command*, without any reaſon aſſigned. That the council did not reſiſt, is true; but this might happen either from inadvertence, or a criminal com-

plaiſance

plaiſance to Lord Mansfield.—You *Barriſters* are too apt to be civil to my Lord Chief Juſtice, at the expence of your clients.

2°. *Junius* did never ſay that Lord Mansfield had *deſtroyed* the liberty of the preſs. "That his lordſhip has *laboured to deſtroy*,— "that his doctrine is an *attack* upon the liberty of the preſs,—that it is an *invaſion* of "the right of juries," are the propoſitions maintained by *Junius*. His opponents never anſwer him in point, for they never meet him fairly upon his own ground.

3°. *Lord Mansfield's* policy, in endeavouring to ſcreen his unconſtitutional doctrines behind an act of the legiſlature, is eaſily underſtood.—Let every Engliſhman ſtand upon his guard;—the right of juries to return a general verdict, in all caſes whatſoever, is a part of our conſtitution. It ſtands in no need of a bill, either *enacting* or *declaratory*, to confirm it.

4°. WITH regard to the *Groſvenor cauſe*, it is pleaſant to obſerve that the doctrine attributed by *Junius* to Lord Mansfield, is admitted by *Zeno* and directly defended. The

Barrister has not the assurance to deny it flatly, but he evades the charge and softens the doctrine by such poor, contemptible quibbles, as cannot impose upon the meanest understanding.

5°. THE quantity of business in the *court of King's Bench* proves nothing but the litigious spirit of the people, arising from the great increase of wealth and commerce. These however are now upon the decline, and will soon leave nothing but *law suits* behind them. When *Junius* affirms that Lord Mansfield has laboured to alter the system of jurisprudence, in the court where his lordship presides, he speaks to those, who are able to look a little farther than the vulgar. Besides that the multitude are easily deceived by the imposing names of *equity* and *substantial justice*, it does not follow that a judge, who introduces into his court new modes of proceeding, and new principles of law, intends, *in every instance*, to decide unjustly. Why should he, where he has no interest?—We say that Lord Mansfield is a bad *man*, and a worse *judge*;—but we do not say that he is a *mere devil*. Our adversaries would fain reduce us to the difficulty of proving too much.—This artifice however ſhall not avail him. The truth of the matter is plainly this. When *Lord Mansfield* has ſucceeded in his ſcheme of changing a court of *common law* to a court of *equity*, he will have it in his power to do injuſtice, *whenever he thinks proper*. This, though a wicked purpoſe, is neither abſurd nor unattainable.

6°. THE laſt paragraph, relative to *Lord Chatham*'s cauſe cannot be anſwered. It partly refers to facts, of too ſecret a nature to be aſcertained and partly is unintelligible. "Upon "*one* point, the cauſe is decided againſt Lord "Chatham.—Upon *another* point, it is de"cided for him."—Both the *law* and the *language* are well ſuited to a *Barriſter!*—If I have any gueſs at this honeſt gentleman's meaning, it is, that, "whereas the com"miſſioners of the Great Seal ſaw the que"ſtion in a point of view unfavourable to "*Lord Chatham*, and decreed accordingly,— "Lord Mansfield, out of ſheer love and kind"neſs to Lord Chatham, took the pains to "place it in a point of view more favourable "to the *appellant*."—*Credat Judæus Apella*. —So curious an aſſertion would ſtagger the faith of *Mr. Sylva*.

LETTER LXIV.

2. *November*, 1771.

WE are desired to make the following declaration, in behalf of *Junius*, upon three material points, on which his opinion has been mistaken, or misrepresented.

1°. *Junius* considers the right of taxing the colonies, by an act of the British Legislature, as a *speculative* right merely, never to be *exerted*, nor ever to be *renounced*. To *his* judgment it appears plain, " That the general " reasonings, which were employed against " that power, went directly to our whole le- " gislative right, and that one part of it could " not be yielded to such arguments, without " a virtual surrender of all the rest."

2°. THAT, with regard to press-warrants, his argument should be taken in his own words, and answered strictly;—that comparisons may sometimes illustrate, but prove nothing; and that, in this case, an appeal to the passions is unfair and unnecessary. *Junius* feels and acknowledges

acknowledges the evil in the moſt expreſs terms, and will ſhew himſelf ready to concur in any rational plan, that may provide for the liberty of the individual, without hazarding the ſafety of the community. At the ſame time, he expects that the evil, ſuch as it is, be not exaggerated or miſrepreſented. In general, it is *not* unjuſt that, when the rich man contributes his wealth, the *poor* man ſhould ſerve the ſtate in perſon;—otherwiſe the latter contributes nothing to the defence of that law and conſtitution, from which he demands ſafety and protection. But the queſtion does not lye between *rich* and *poor*. The laws of England make no ſuch diſtinctions. Neither is it true that the poor man is torn from the care and ſupport of a wiſe and family, helpleſs without him. The ſingle queſtion is, whether the *ſeaman**, in times of public danger, ſhall ſerve the merchant or the ſtate, in that profeſſion to which he was bred, and by the exerciſe of which alone he can honeſtly ſupport himſelf and his family.—General arguments againſt the doctrine of *neceſſity*, and the dangerous uſe that may be made of it, are of no

* I confine myſelf ſtrictly to *ſeamen*;—if any others are preſſed, it is a groſs abuſe, which the magiſtrate can and ſhould correct.

weight

weight in this particular caſe. *Neceſſity* includes the idea of *inevitable*. Whenever it is ſo, it creates a law, to which all *poſitive* laws, and all *poſitive* rights muſt give way. In this ſenſe the levy of *ſhip-money* by the King's warrant was not *neceſſary*, becauſe the buſineſs might have been as well or better done by parliament. If the doctrine, maintained by *Junius*, be confined within this limitation, it will go but very little way in ſupport of arbitrary power. That the King is to judge of the occaſion, is no objection, unleſs we are told how it can poſſibly be otherwiſe. There are other inſtances, not leſs important in the exerciſe nor leſs dangerous in the abuſe, in which the conſtitution relies entirely upon the King's judgment. The executive power proclaims war and peace, binds the nation by treaties, orders general embargoes, and impoſes quarantines, not to mention a multitude of prerogative writs, which, though liable to the greateſt abuſes, were never diſputed.

3°. IT has been urged, as a reproach to *Junius*, that he has not delivered an opinion upon the Game Laws, and particularly the late *Dog-act*. But *Junius* thinks he has much greater reaſon to complain, that he is never

aſſiſted

aſſiſted by thoſe, who are able to aſſiſt him, and that almoſt the whole labour of the preſs is thrown upon a ſingle hand, from which a diſcuſſion of *every* public queſtion whatſoever is unreaſonably expected. He is not paid for his labour, and certainly has a right to chooſe his employment.——As to the *Game Laws*, he never ſcrupled to declare his opinion, that they are a ſpecies of the *Foreſt Laws*, that they are oppreſſive to the ſubject, and that the ſpirit of them is incompatible with legal liberty:—that the penalties, impoſed by theſe laws, bear no proportion to the nature of the offence, that the mode of trial and the degree and kind of evidence neceſſary to convict, not only deprive the ſubject of all the benefits of a trial by jury, but are in themſelves too ſummary, and to the laſt degree arbitrary and oppreſſive. That, in particular, the late acts to prevent dog-ſtealing, or killing game between ſun and ſun, are diſtinguiſhed by their abſurdity, extravagance, and pernicious tendency. If theſe terms are weak, or ambiguous, in what language can *Junius* expreſs himſelf? —It is no excuſe for *Lord Mansfield* to ſay that he *happened* to be abſent when theſe bills paſſed the houſe of lords. It was his duty to be preſent. Such bills could never have paſſed

the

the house of commons without his knowledge. But we very well know by what rule he regulates his attendance. When that order was made in the house of lords in the case of *Lord Pomfret*, at which every Englishman shudders, my honest *Lord Mansfield* found himself, *by mere accident*, in the court of king's bench.—Otherwise, he would have done wonders in defence of law and property! The pitiful evasion is adapted to the character. But *Junius* will never justify himself, by the example of this bad man. The distinction between *doing wrong*, and *avoiding to do right* belongs to Lord Mansfield. *Junius* disclaims it.

LETTER LXV.

TO LORD CHIEF JUSTICE MANSFIELD.

2. *November*, 1771.

AT the intercession of three of your countrymen, you have bailed a man, who, I presume, is also a *Scotchman*, and whom the Lord Mayor of London had refused to bail. I do not mean to enter into an examination of the partial, sinister motives of your conduct;

conduct; but confining myself strictly to the fact, I affirm, that you have done that, which by law you were not warranted to do. The thief was taken in the theft;—the stolen goods were found upon him, and he made no defence. In these circumstances, (the truth of which You dare not deny, because it is of public notoriety) it could not stand indifferent whether he was guilty or not, much less could there be any presumption of his innocence; and, in these circumstances, I affirm, in contradiction to YOU, LORD CHIEF JUSTICE MANSFIELD, that, by the laws of England, he was *not bailable*. If ever *Mr. Eyre* should be brought to trial, we shall hear what You have to say for Yourself; and I pledge myself, before God and my country, in proper time and place to make good my charge against you.

JUNIUS.

LETTER LXVI.

TO THE PRINTER OF THE PUBLIC ADVERTISER.

9. *November* 1771.

JUNIUS engages to make good his charge againſt *Lord Chief Juſtice Mansfield*, ſome time before the meeting of parliament, in order that the houſe of commons may, if they think proper, make it one article in the impeachment of the ſaid *Lord Chief Juſtice.*

LETTER LXVII.

TO HIS GRACE THE DUKE OF GRAFTON.

27. *Nov.* 1771.

WHAT is the reaſon, my Lord, that, when almoſt every man in the kingdom, without diſtinction of principles or party, exults in the ridiculous defeat of Sir James Lowther, when good and bad men unite in one common opinion of that baronet, and triumph in his diſtreſs, as if the event

event (without any reference to vice or virtue) were interesting to human nature, your Grace alone should appear so miserably depressed and afflicted? In such universal joy, I know not where you will look for a compliment of condoleance, unless you appeal to the tender, sympathetic sorrows of Mr. Bradshaw. That cream-coloured gentleman's tears, affecting as they are, carry consolation along with them. He never weeps, but, like an April shower, with a lambent ray of sunshine upon his countenance. From the feelings of honest men, upon this joyful occasion, I do not mean to draw any conclusion to your Grace. *They* naturally rejoice, when they see a signal instance of tyranny resisted with success;—of treachery exposed to the derision of the world;—an infamous informer defeated, and an impudent robber dragged to the public gibbet.—But, in the *other* class of mankind, I own I expected to meet the Duke of Grafton. Men, who have no regard for justice, nor any sense of honour, seem as heartily pleased with Sir James Lowther's well deserved punishment, as if it did not constitute an example against themselves. The unhappy Baronet has no friends, even among those

who

who reſemble him. You, my Lord, are not reduced to ſo deplorable a ſtate of dereliction. Every villain in the kingdom is your friend; and, in compliment to ſuch amity, I think you ſhould ſuffer your diſmal countenance to clear up. Beſides, my Lord;—I am a little anxious for the conſiſtency of your character. You violate your own rules of decorum, when you do not inſult the man, whom you have betrayed.

THE divine juſtice of retribution ſeems now to have begun its progreſs. Deliberate treachery entails puniſhment upon the traitor. There is no poſſibility of eſcaping it, even in the higheſt rank, to which the conſent of ſociety can exalt the meaneſt and worſt of men. The forced, unnatural union of Luttrell a..d Middleſex was an omen of ano.her unnatural union, by which indefeaſible infamy is attached to the houſe of Brunſwick. If one of thoſe acts was virtuous and honourable, the beſt of princes, I thank God, is happily rewarded for it by the other. —Your Grace, *it has been ſaid*, had ſome ſhare in recommending Colonel Luttrell to the King;—or was it only the gentle Bradſhaw, who made himſelf anſwerable for the good

good behaviour of his friend? An intimate connexion has long subsisted between him and the worthy Lord Irnham. It arose from a fortunate similarity of principles, cemented by the constant mediation of their common friend Miss Davis *.

YET

* There is a certain family in this country, on which nature seems to have entailed an hereditary baseness of disposition. As far as their history has been known, the son has regularly improved upon the vices of his father, and has taken care to transmit them pure and undiminished into the bosom of his successor. In the senate, their abilities have confined them to those humble, sordid services, in which the scavengers of the ministry are usually employed. But in the memoirs of private treachery, they stand first and unrivalled. The following story will serve to illustrate the character of this respectable family, and to convince the world that the present possessor has as clear a title to the infamy of his ancestors, as he has to their estate. It deserves to be recorded for the curiosity of the fact, and should be given to the public as a warning to every honest member of society.

The present Lord Irnham, who is now in the decline of life, lately cultivated the acquaintance of a younger brother of a family, with which he had lived in some degree of intimacy and friendship. The young man had long been the dupe of a most unhappy attachment to a common prostitute. His friends and relations foresaw the consequences of this connexion, and did every thing that depended upon them to save him from ruin. But he had a friend in Lord Irnham, whose advice rendered all their endeavours ineffectual. This hoary letcher, not contented with the enjoyment of his friend's mistress, was base enough to take advantage of the passions and folly of a young man, and persuaded him to marry her.

 He

Yet I confeſs I ſhould be ſorry that the opprobrious infamy of this match ſhould reach beyond the family.—We have now a better reaſon than ever to pray for the long life of the beſt of princes, and the welfare of his royal *iſſue*.—I will not mix any thing ominous with my prayers;—but let parliament look to it.—A *Luttrell* ſhall never ſucceed to the crown of England.—If the hereditary virtues of the family deſerve a kingdom, Scotland will be a proper retreat for them.

The next is a moſt remarkable inſtance of the goodneſs of providence. The juſt law of retaliation has at laſt overtaken the little, contemptible tyrant of the North. To this ſon-in-law of your deareſt friend the Earl of Bute, you meant to transfer the Duke of Portland's property; and you haſtened the grant, with an expedition unknown to the

He deſcended even to perform the office of father to the proſtitute. He gave her to his friend, who was on the point of leaving the kingdom, and the next night lay with her himſelf.

Whether the depravity of the human heart can produce any thing more baſe and deteſtable than this fact, muſt be left undetermined, until the ſon ſhall arrive at his father's age and experience.

Treaſury,

Treaſury, that he might have it time enough to give a deciſive turn to the election for the county. The immediate conſequence of this flagitious robbery was, that he loſt the election, which you meant to inſure to him, and with ſuch ſignal circumſtances of ſcorn, reproach, and inſult, (to ſay nothing of the general exultation of all parties) as, (excepting the King's brother-in-law Col. Luttrell, and old *Simon* his father-in-law) hardly ever fell upon a gentleman in this country.—In the event, he loſes the very property, of which he thought he had gotten poſſeſſion; and after an expence, which would have paid the value of the land in queſtion twenty times over.---The forms of villainy, you ſee, are neceſſary to its ſucceſs. Hereafter you will act with greater circumſpection, and not drive ſo directly to your object. To *ſnatch a grace*, beyond the reach of common treachery, is an exception, not a rule.

AND now, my good Lord, does not your conſcious heart inform you, that the juſtice of retribution begins to operate, and that it may ſoon approach your perſon?—Do you think that *Junius* has renounced the Middleſex election?—Or that the King's timber ſhall be refuſed to the Royal Navy with impunity?—Or that you ſhall hear no more of the ſale of that patent to *Mr. Hine*, which you endeavoured to ſkreen by ſuddenly dropping your proſecution of *Samuel Vaughan*, when the rule againſt him was made abſolute? I believe indeed there never was ſuch an inſtance in all the hiſtory of negative impudence.—But it ſhall not ſave you. The very ſunſhine you live in is a prelude to your diſſolution. When you are ripe, you ſhall be plucked.

JUNIUS.

P. S. I beg you will convey to our gracious maſter my humble congratulations upon the glorious ſucceſs of peerages and penſions, ſo laviſhly diſtributed as the rewards of Iriſh virtue.

LETTER LXVIII.

TO LORD CHIEF JUSTICE MANSFIELD.

21. *January*, 1772.

I HAVE undertaken to prove that when, at the interceſſion of three of your countrymen, you bailed *John Eyre*, you did that, *which by law you were not warranted to do*, and that a felon, under the circumſtances, *of being taken in the fact, with the ſtolen goods upon him, and making no defence*, is *not bailable* by the laws of England. Your learned advocates have interpreted this charge into a denial that the court of King's Bench, or the judges of that court during the vacation, have any greater authority to bail for criminal offences, than a juſtice of peace. With the inſtance before me, I am ſuppoſed to queſtion your power of doing wrong, and to deny the exiſtence of a power, at the ſame moment that I arraign the illegal exerciſe of it. But the opinions of ſuch men, whether wilful in their malignity, or ſincere in their ignorance, are unworthy of my notice. You,

Lord Mansfield, did not underſtand me ſo, and, I promiſe you, your cauſe requires an abler defence.—I am now to make good my charge againſt you. However dull my argument, the ſubject of it is intereſting. I ſhall be honoured with the attention of the public, and have a right to demand the attention of the legiſlature. Supported, as I am, by the whole body of the criminal law of England, I have no doubt of eſtabliſhing my charge. If, on your part, you ſhould have no plain, ſubſtantial defence, but ſhould endeavour to ſhelter yourſelf under the quirk and evaſion of a practiſing lawyer, or under the mere, inſulting aſſertion of power without right, the reputation you pretend to is gone for ever;—you ſtand degraded from the reſpect and authority of your office, and are no longer, *de jure*, Lord Chief Juſtice of England. This letter, my Lord, is addreſſed, not ſo much to *you*, as to the public. Learned as you are, and quick in apprehenſion, few arguments are neceſſary to ſatisfy you, that you have done that, which by law you were not warranted to do. Your conſcience already tells you, that you have ſinned againſt knowledge, and that whatever defence you make contradicts your own internal conviction. But other men are wil-

ling

ling enough to take the law upon truſt. They rely upon your authority, becauſe they are too indolent to ſearch for information; or, conceiving that there is ſome myſtery in the laws of their country, which lawyers only are qualified to explain, they diſtruſt their judgment, and voluntarily renounce the right of thinking for themſelves. With all the evidence of hiſtory before them, from *Treſillian* to *Jefferies*, from *Jefferies* to *Mansfield*, they will not believe it poſſible that a learned judge can act in direct contradiction to thoſe laws, which he is ſuppoſed to have made the ſtudy of his life, and which he has ſworn to adminiſter faithfully. Superſtition is certainly not the characteriſtic of this age. Yet ſome men are bigoted in politics, who are infidels in religion. —I do not deſpair of making them aſhamed of their credulity.

THE charge I brought againſt you is expreſſed in terms guarded and well conſidered. They do not deny the ſtrict power of the judges of the court of King's Bench to bail in caſes, not bailable by a juſtice of peace, nor repleviſable by the common writ, or *ex officio* by the Sheriff. I well knew the practice of the court, and by what legal rules it ought to be directed. But, far from meaning to soften or diminish the force of those terms I have made use of, I now go beyond them, and affirm,

I. THAT the superior power of bailing for felony, claimed by the court of King's Bench, is founded upon the opinion of lawyers, and the practice of the court;—that the assent of the legislature to this power is merely negative, and that it is not supported by any positive provision in any statute whatsoever.—If it be, produce the statute.

II. ADMITTING that the judges of the court of King's Bench are vested with a discretionary power to examine and judge of circumstances and allegations, which a justice of peace is not permitted to consider, I affirm that the judges, in the use and application of that discretionary power, are as strictly bound by the spirit, intent, and meaning, as the justice of peace is by the words of the legislature. Favourable circumstances, alledged before the judge, may justify a doubt whether the prisoner be guilty or not; and where the guilt is doubtful, a presumption of innocence should, in general, be admitted. But, when any

any ſuch probable circumſtances are alledged, they alter the ſtate and condition of the priſoner. *He* is no longer that *all-but-convicted* felon, whom the law intends, and who by law is *not bailable at all.* If no circumſtances whatſoever are alledged in his favour ;—if no allegation whatſoever be made to leſſen the force of that evidence, which the law annexes to a poſitive charge of felony, and particularly to the fact of *being taken with the maner*, I then ſay that the Lord Chief Juſtice of England has no more right to bail him than a juſtice of peace. The diſcretion of an Engliſh judge is not of mere will and pleaſure ;—it is not arbitrary ;—it is not capricious ; but, as that great lawyer, (whoſe authority I wiſh you reſpected half as much as I do) truly ſays *, " Diſcretion, taken as it ought to be, is, *diſ-* " *cernere per legem quid ſit juſtum.* If it be " not directed by the right line of the law, " it is a crooked cord, and appeareth to be " unlawful."—If diſcretion were arbitrary in the judge, he might introduce whatever novelties he thought proper ; but, ſays Lord Coke, " Novelties, without warrant of pre- " cedents, are not to be allowed ; ſome cer-

* 4. *Inſt.* 41. 66.

" tain

"tain rules are to be followed;—*Quicquid* "*judicis authoritati ſubjicitur, novitati non ſub-*"*jicitur*;" and this ſound doctrine is applied to the Star-chamber, a court confeſſedly arbitrary. If you will abide by the authority of this great man, you ſhall have all the advantage of his opinion, wherever it appears to favour you. Excepting the plain, expreſs meaning of the legiſlature, to which all private opinions muſt give way, I deſire no better judge between us than Lord Coke.

III. I AFFIRM that, according to the obvious, indiſputable meaning of the legiſlature, repeatedly expreſſed, a perſon poſitively charged with *feloniouſly ſtealing* and taken *in flagrante delicto*, with the ſtolen goods upon him, is *not bailable*. The law conſiders him as differing in nothing from a *convict*, but in the form of conviction, and (whatever a corrupt judge may do) will accept of no ſecurity, but the confinement of his body within four walls. I know it has been alledged in your favour, that you have often bailed for murders, rapes, and other manifeſt crimes. Without queſtioning the fact, I ſhall not admit that you are to be juſtified by your own example. If that were a protection to you, where is the crime that, as a judge,

judge, you might not now securely commit? But neither shall I suffer myself to be drawn aside from my present argument, nor *you* to profit by your own wrong.—To prove the meaning and intent of the legislature will require a minute and tedious deduction. To investigate a question of law demands some labour and attention, though very little genius or sagacity. As a practical profession, the study of the law requires but a moderate portion of abilities. The learning of a pleader is usually upon a level with his integrity. The indiscriminate defence of right and wrong contracts the understanding, while it corrupts the heart. Subtlety is soon mistaken for wisdom, and impunity for virtue. If there be any instances upon record, as some there are undoubtedly, of genius and morality united in a lawyer, they are distinguished by their singularity, and operate as exceptions.

I MUST solicit the patience of my readers. This is no light matter, nor is it any more susceptible of ornament, than the conduct of Lord Mansfield is capable of aggravation.

As the law of bail, in charges of felony, has been exactly ascertained by acts of the legislature, it is at present of little consequence to enquire how it stood at common law, before the statute of Westminster. And yet it is worth the reader's attention to observe, how nearly, in the ideas of our ancestors, the circumstance of being taken *with the maner* approached to the conviction of the felon *. It "fixed the authoritative stamp "of verisimilitude upon the accusation, and, "by the common law, when a thief was "taken *with the maner* (that is, with the "thing stolen upon him, *in manu)* he might, "so detected *flagrante delicto*, be brought in-"to court, arraigned and tried, *without in-"dictment*; as, by the Danish law, he might "be taken and hanged upon the spot, with-"out accusation or trial." It will soon appear that our statute law, in this behalf, tho' less summary in point of proceeding, is directed by the same spirit. In one instance, the very form is adhered to. In offences relating to the forest, if a man was taken with vert, or venison †, it was declared to be equivalent

* *Blackstone*, 4. 303.

† 1 *Ed*. III. *cap*. 8.---and 7 *Rich*. II. *cap*. 4.

to

to indictment. To enable the reader to judge for himself, I shall state, in due order, the several statutes relative to bail in criminal cases, or as much of them as may be material to the point in question, omitting superfluous words. If I misrepresent, or do not quote with fidelity, it will not be difficult to detect me.

* THE statute of Westminster the first, in 1275, sets forth that, "Forasmuch as "Sheriffs and others, who have taken and "kept in prison persons detected of felony, "and incontinent have let out by replevin "such as were *not replevisable* because they "would gain of the one party and grieve the "other; and, forasmuch as, before this "time, it was not determined which per- "sons were replevisable and which not, it is "provided and by the King commanded that "such prisoners, &c. as be *taken with the ma- "ner*, &c. or for *manifest* offences, shall be "*in no wise* replevisable by the common "writ, nor without writ." † —Lord Coke, in

* "*Videtur que le statute de mainprise nest que reversall del "comen ley.*" Bro. Mainp. 61.

† "There are three points to be considered in the con- "struction of all remedial statutes;---the old law, the mis- "chief,

in his exposition of the last part of this quotation, accurately distinguishes between *replevy* by the common writ or ex officio, and *bail* by the King's Bench. The words of the statute certainly do not extend to the judges of that court. But, besides that the reader will soon find reason to think that the legislature, in their intention, made no difference between *bailable* and *replevisable*, Lord Coke himself (if he be understood to mean nothing but an exposition of the statute of Westminster, and not to state the law generally) does not adhere to his own distinction. In expounding the other offences, which, by this statute, are declared *not replevisable*, he constantly uses the words *not bailable*.—— "That outlaws, for instance, are *not bailable at all*;—that persons, who have abjured the realm, are attainted upon their own confession, and therefore *not bailable at all by law*;—that provers are *not bail-*

"chief, and the remedy;---that is, how the common law stood at the making of the act, what the mischief was for which the common law did not provide, and what remedy the parliament hath provided to cure this mischief. It is the business of the judges, so to construe the act, as to suppress the mischief and advance the remedy."

Blackstone, 1. 87.

"*able*;

" *able*;—that notorious felons are *not bail-*
" *able.*" The reaſon, why the ſuperior courts were not named in the ſtatute of Weſt-minſter, was plainly this, " becauſe antient-
" ly moſt of the buſineſs, touching bailment
" of priſoners for felony or miſdemeanors,
" was performed by the Sheriffs, or ſpecial
" bailiffs of liberties, either by writ, or *virtute*
" *officii* *;" conſequently the ſuperior courts had little or no opportunity to commit thoſe abuſes, which the ſtatute imputes to the Sheriffs.—With ſubmiſſion to Doctor Black-ſtone, I think he has fallen into a contra-diction, which, in terms at leaſt, appears ir-reconcileable. After enumerating ſeveral offences not bailable, he aſſerts, without any condition or limitation whatſoever †,
" all theſe are clearly not admiſſible to bail." Yet in a few lines after he ſays, " *it is*
" *agreed* that the court of King's Bench may
" bail for any crime whatſoever, *according to*
" *circumſtances of* the caſe." To his firſt pro-poſition he ſhould have added, *by Sheriffs or Juſtices*; otherwiſe the two propoſitions contradict each other; with this difference however, that the firſt is abſolute, the ſecond

* 2 *Hale*, P. C. 128. 136.

† *Blackſtone*, 4. 296.

limited

limited by *a consideration of circumstances.* I say this without the least intended disrespect to the learned author. His work is of public utility, and should not hastily be condemned.

THE statute of 17 *Richard* II. *cap.* 10. 1393, sets forth, that "forasmuch as "thieves notoriously defamed, *and others* "*taken with the maner*, by their long abiding "in prison, were delivered by charters, and "favourable inquests procured, to the great "hindrance of the people, two men of law "shall be assigned, in every commission of "the peace, to proceed to the deliverance "of such felons, &c." It seems by this act, that there was a constant struggle between the legislature and the officers of justice. Not daring to admit felons *taken with the maner* to bail or mainprize, they evaded the law by keeping the party in prison a long time, and then delivering him without due trial.

THE statute of 1 *Richard* III. in 1483, sets forth, that "forasmuch as divers persons "have been daily arrested and imprisoned for "*suspicion* of felony, sometime of malice, and "sometime of *a light suspicion*, and so kept in "prison without bail or mainprize, be it or-

"dained

"dained that every justice of peace shall have "authority, by his discretion, to let such "prisoners and persons so arrested to bail or "mainprize."—By this act it appears that there had been abuses in matter of imprisonment, and that the legislature meant to provide for the immediate enlargement of persons arrested on *light suspicion* of felony.

The statute of 3 Henry VII. in 1486, declares, that "under colour of the preceding act of Richard the Third, persons, "*such as were not mainpernable*, were oftentimes let to bail or mainprize, by justices "of the peace, whereby many murderers and "felons escaped, the King, &c. hath ordained, that the justices of the peace, or "two of them at least (whereof one to be "of the *quorum*) have authority to let any "such prisoners or persons, mainpernable by "the law, to bail or mainprize."

The statute of 1st and 2d of Philip and Mary, in 1554, sets forth, that "notwithstanding the preceding statute of Henry "the Seventh, *one* justice of peace hath oftentimes, by sinister labour and means, set "at large the greatest and notablest offenders,

"*such as be not replevisable by the laws of this*
"*realm*, and yet, the rather to hide their
"affections in that behalf, have signed
"the cause of their apprehension to be but
"only for *suspicion* of felony, whereby the
"said offenders have escaped unpunished,
"and do daily, to the high displeasure of
"Almighty God, the great peril of the King
"and Queen's true subjects, and encourage-
"ment of all thieves and evil-doers;—for
"reformation whereof be it enacted, that no
"justices of peace shall let to bail or main-
"prize any such persons, which, for any
"offence by them committed, be declared *not*
"to be *replevised*, or *bailed*, or be forbidden
"to be *replevised* or *bailed* by the statute of
"Westminster the first; and furthermore
"that any persons, arrested for manslaughter,
"felony, *being bailable by the law*, shall not
"be let to bail or mainprize, by any justices
"of peace, but in the form therein after
"prescribed."—In the two preceding statutes, the words *bailable*, *replevisable*, and
mainpernable are used synonymously *, or
promiscuously to express the same single intention of the legislature, viz. *not to accept of*

* 2 *Hale*, P. C. 2. 124.

any

any ſecurity but the body of the offender ; and when the latter ſtatute preſcribes the form, in which perſons arreſted on *ſuſpicion* of felony *(being bailable by the law)* may be let to bail, it evidently ſuppoſes that there are ſome caſes, *not* bailable by the law.—It may be thought perhaps, that I attribute to the legiſlature an appearance of inaccuracy in the uſe of terms, merely to ſerve my preſent purpoſe. But, in truth, it would make more forcibly for my argument to preſume that the legiſlature were conſtantly aware of the ſtrict legal diſtinction between *bail* and *replevy*, and that they always meant to adhere to it *. For if it be true that *replevy* is by the Sheriffs, and *bail* by the higher courts at Weſtminſter, (which I think no lawyer will deny) it follows that, when the legiſlature expreſsly ſay, that any particular offence is by law *not bailable*, the ſuperior courts are comprehended in the prohibition, and bound by it. Otherwiſe, unleſs there was a poſitive exception of the ſuperior courts (which I af-

* *Vide* 2 Inſt. 150. 186.---" The word *repleviſable* never " ſignifies *bailable*. *Bailable* is in a court of record by the " King's juſtices; but *repleviſable* is by the Sheriff."

Selden, State Tr. 7. 149.

firm there never was in any ſtatute relative to bail) the legiſlature would groſsly contradict themſelves, and the manifeſt intention of the law be evaded. It is an eſtabliſhed rule that, when the law is *ſpecial*, and reaſon of it general, it is to be *generally* underſtood; and though, by cuſtom, a latitude be allowed to the court of King's Bench, (to conſider circumſtances inductive of a doubt whether the priſoner be guilty or innocent) if this latitude be taken as an arbitrary power to bail, when no circumſtances whatſoever are alledged in favour of the priſoner, it is a power without right, and a daring violation of the whole Engliſh law of bail.

THE act of the 31ſt of Charles the Second (commonly called the *Habeas Corpus act*) particularly declares, that it is not meant to extend to treaſon or felony plainly and ſpecially expreſſed in the warrant of commitment. The priſoner is therefore left to ſeek his *Habeas Corpus* at common law; and ſo far was the legiſlature from ſuppoſing that perſons, (committed for treaſon or felony plainly and ſpecially expreſſed in the warrant of commitment) could be let to bail by a ſingle

ſingle judge, or by the whole court, that this very act provides a remedy for ſuch perſons, in caſe they are not indicted in the courſe of the term or ſeſſions ſubſequent to their commitment. The law neither ſuffers them to be enlarged before trial, nor to be impriſoned after the time, in which they ought regularlarly to be tried. In this caſe the law ſays, "It ſhall and may be lawful to and for the "judges of the court of King's Bench and "juſtices of oyer and terminer, or general "goal delivery, and they are hereby re-"quired, upon motion to them made in open "court, the laſt day of the term, ſeſſion, "or goal delivery, either by the priſoner or "any one in his behalf, to ſet at liberty the "priſoner upon bail; unleſs it appear to the "judges and juſtices, upon oath made, that "the witneſſes for the King could not be "produced the ſame term, ſeſſions, or goal "delivery,"—Upon the whole of this article I obſerve, 1. That the proviſion, made in the firſt part of it, would be, in a great meaſure, uſeleſs and nugatory, if any ſingle judge might have bailed the priſoner *ex arbitrio*, during the vacation; or if the court might have bailed him immediately after the commencement of the term or ſeſſions.——

 2. When

2. When the law ſays, *It ſhall and may be lawful* to bail for felony under particular circumſtances, we muſt preſume that, before the paſſing of that act, it was *not* lawful to bail under thoſe circumſtances. The terms uſed by the legiſlature are *enacting*, not *declaratory*. — 3. Notwithſtanding the party may have been impriſoned during the greateſt part of the vacation, and during the whole ſeſſion, the court are expreſsly forbidden to bail him from that ſeſſion to the next, if oath be made that the witneſſes for the King could not be produced that ſame term or ſeſſions.

HAVING faithfully ſtated the ſeveral acts of parliament relative to bail in criminal caſes, it may be uſeful to the reader to take a ſhort, hiſtorical review of the law of bail, through its various gradations and improvements.

BY the ancient common law, before and ſince the conqueſt, all felonies were bailable, till murder was excepted by ſtatute, ſo that perſons might be admitted to bail, before conviction, almoſt in every caſe. The ſtatute of Weſtminſter ſays that, before that time,

time, it had not been determined, which offences were replevisable, and which were not, whether by the common writ *de homine replegiando*, or *ex officio* by the Sheriff. It is very remarkable that the abuses arising from this unlimited power of replevy, dreadful as they were and destructive to the peace of society, were not corrected or taken notice of by the legislature, until the commons of the kingdom had obtained a share in it by their representatives; but the house of commons had scarce begun to exist, when these formidable abuses were corrected by the statute of Westminster. It is highly probable that the mischief had been severely felt by the people, although no remedy had been provided for it by the Norman Kings or Barons. * "The "iniquity of the times was so great, as it "even forced the subjects to forego that, "which was in account a great liberty, to "stop the course of a growing mischief." The preamble to the statutes, made by the first parliament of Edward the First, assigns the reason of calling it, † "because the peo"ple had been otherwise entreated than they "ought to be, the peace less kept, the laws

* *Selden*, by *N. Bacon*. 182.

† Parliamentary History. 1. 82.

"less used, and *offenders less punished* than they
" ought to be, by reason whereof the people
" feared less to offend;" and the first attempt
to reform these various abuses was by contracting the power of replevying felons.

For above two centuries following it does not appear that any alteration was made in the law of bail, except that *being taken with vert or venison* was declared to be equivalent to indictment. The legislature adhered firmly to the spirit of the statute of Westminster. The statute of 27th of Edward the first directs the justices of assize to enquire and punish officers bailing such as were *not bailable*. As for the judges of the superior courts, it is probable that, in those days, they thought themselves bound by the obvious intent and meaning of the legislature. They considered not so much to what particular persons the prohibition was addressed, as what the *thing* was, which the legislature meant to prohibit, well knowing that in law, *quando aliquid prohibetur, prohibetur et omne, per quod devenitur ad illud.* " When any thing is forbidden, all the means,
" by which the same thing may be compassed
" or done, are equally forbidden."

By

By the ſtatute of Richard the third, the power of bailing was a little enlarged. Every juſtice of peace was authoriſed to bail for felony; but they were expreſsly confined to perſons arreſted *on light ſuſpicion*; and even this power, ſo limited, was found to produce ſuch inconveniences that, in three years after, the legiſlature found it neceſſary to repeal it. Inſtead of truſting any longer to a ſingle juſtice of peace, the act of 3d. Henry VIIth, repeals the preceding act, and directs "that "no priſoner, *(of thoſe who are mainpernable "by the law)* ſhall be let to bail or mainpriſe, "by leſs than *two* juſtices, whereof one to be "of the quorum." And ſo indiſpenſably neceſſary was this proviſion thought, for the adminiſtration of juſtice, and for the ſecurity and peace of ſociety, that, at this time, an oath was propoſed by the King to be taken by the knights and eſquires of his houſehold, by the members of the houſe of commons, and by the peers ſpiritual and temporal, and accepted and ſworn to *quaſi unâ voce* by them all, which, among other engagements, binds them "not to let any man to "bail or mainpriſe, knowing and deeming him

"him to be a felon, upon your honour and
"worſhip. So help you God and all ſaints.*"

In about half a century however even theſe proviſions were found inſufficient. The act of Henry the ſeventh was evaded, and the legiſlature once more obliged to interpoſe. The act of 1ſt and 2d of Philip and Mary takes away intirely from the juſtices all power of bailing for offences declared *not bailable* by the ſtatute of Weſtminſter.

THE illegal impriſonment of ſeveral perſons, who had refuſed to contribute to a loan exacted by Charles the firſt, and the delay of the *Habeas Corpus* and ſubſequent refuſal to bail them, conſtituted one of the firſt and moſt important grievances of that reign. Yet when the houſe of commons, which met in the year 1628, reſolved upon meaſures of the moſt firm and ſtrenuous reſiſtance to the power of impriſonment aſſumed by the King or privy-council, and to the refuſal to bail the party on the return of the *Habeas Corpus*, they did expreſsly, in all their reſolutions, make an exception of commitments, where the cauſe

* Parliamentary Hiſtory. 2. 419.

of the reſtraint was expreſſed, and did by law juſtify the commitment. The reaſon of the diſtinction is, that, whereas when the cauſe of commitment is expreſſed, the crime is then known and the offender muſt be brought to the ordinary trial; if, on the contrary, no cauſe of commitment be expreſſed, and the priſoner be thereupon remanded, it may operate to perpetual impriſonment. This conteſt with Charles the firſt produced the act of the 16th of that King, by which the court of King's Bench are directed, within three days after the return to the *Habeas Corpus* to examine and determine the legality of any commitment by the King or privy-council, and to do *what to juſtice ſhall appertain* in delivering, bailing, or *remanding* the priſoner.—*Now*, it ſeems, it is unneceſſary for the judge to do what appertains to juſtice. The ſame ſcandalous traffic, in which we have ſeen the privilege of parliament exerted or relaxed, to gratify the preſent humour, or to ſerve the immediate purpoſe of the crown, is introduced into the adminiſtration of juſtice. The magiſtrate, it ſeems, has now no rule to follow, but the dictates of perſonal enmity, national partiality, or perhaps the moſt proſtituted corruption.

To compleat this historical inquiry, it only remains to be observed that, the *Habeas Corpus* act of 31st of Charles the second, so justly considered as another Magna Carta of the kingdom * "extends only to the case of com-"mitments for such criminal charge, as can "produce no inconvenience to public justice "by a temporary enlargement of the pri-"soner."—So careful were the legislature, at the very moment, when they were providing for the liberty of the subject, not to furnish any colour or pretence for violating or evading the established law of bail in the higher criminal offences. But the exception, stated in the body of the act, puts the matter out of all doubt. After directing the judges how they are to proceed to the discharge of the prisoner upon recognisance and surety, having regard to the quality of the prisoner and nature of the offence, it is expressly added, "unless it "shall appear to the said Lord Chancellor, "&c. that the party, so committed, is detained "for such matters, or offences, for the which, "BY THE LAW THE PRISONER IS NOT "BAILABLE."

* Blackstone. 4. 137.

WHEN

When the laws, plain of themſelves, are thus illuſtrated by facts, and their uniform meaning eſtabliſhed by hiſtory we do not want the authority of opinions however reſpectable, to inform our judgment or to confirm our belief. But I am determined that you ſhall have no eſcape. Authority of every ſort ſhall be produced againſt you, from *Jacob* to *Lord Coke*, from the dictionary to the claſſic.—In vain ſhall you appeal from thoſe upright judges, whom you diſdain to imitate, to thoſe whom you have made your example. With one voice, they all condemn you.

"To be taken with the *maner* is where a "thief, having ſtolen any thing, is taken "with the ſame about him, as it were in his "hands, which is called *flagrante delicto*. "Such a criminal is *not bailable by law*."—*Jacob under the word Maner.*

"Those, who are taken with the *Maner*, "are excluded, by the ſtatute of Weſtmin-"ſter, from the benefit of a replevin."—*Hawkins. P. C.* 2. 98.

"Of

" OF ſuch heinous offences no one, who is
" notoriouſly guilty, ſeems to be *bailable* by
" the intent of this ſtatute."—*D*°. 2. 99.

" THE common practice, and allowed ge-
" neral rule is, that bail is only then proper
" where it ſtands *indifferent* whether the party
" were guilty or innocent."—*D*°. *D*°.

" THERE is no doubt but that the bailing
" of a perſon, *who is not bailable by law*, is
" puniſhable, either at common law as a neg-
" ligent eſcape, or as an offence againſt the
" ſeveral ſtatutes relative to bail."—*D*°. 89.

" IT cannot be doubted but that, neither the
" judges of this, nor of any other ſuperior court
" of juſtice, are ſtrictly within the purview
" of that ſtatute, yet they will always, in their
" diſcretion, pay a due regard to it, and not
" admit a perſon to bail, who is expreſsly
" declared by it irreplevisable, *without ſome*
" *particular circumſtance in his favour*; and
" therefore it ſeems difficult to find an inſtance,
" where perſons, attainted of felony, or noto-
" riouſly guilty of treaſon or manſlaughter,
" &c. by their own confeſſion, or *otherwiſe*,
" have

" have been admitted to the benefit of bail, " without ſome ſpecial motive to the court to " grant it."—*D°*. 114.

" If it appears that any man hath injury " or wrong by his impriſonment, we have " power to deliver and diſcharge him;—if " otherwiſe, *he is to be remanded* by us to " priſon again."—*Lord Ch. J. Hyde. State Trials*. 7. 115.

" The ſtatute of Weſtminſter was eſpe- " cially for direction to the Sheriffs and " others, but to ſay courts of juſtice are ex- " cluded from this ſtatute, I conceive it can- " not be."—*Attorney General Heath. D°*. 132.

" The court, upon view of the return, " judgeth of the ſufficiency or inſufficiency " of it. If they think the priſoner *in law* to " be *bailable*, he is committed to the Marſhal " and bailed; if not, he is remanded."— Through the whole debate the objection, on the part of the priſoners, was, that no cauſe of commitment was expreſſed in the warrant; but it was uniformly admitted by their council that, if the cauſe of commitment had been expreſſed

expressed for treason or felony, the court would then have done right in remanding them.

THE Attorney General having urged, before a committee of both houses, that, in Beckwith's case and others, the lords of the council sent a letter to the court of King's Bench to bail; it was replied by the managers of the house of commons, that this was of no moment, "for that either the prisoner "was *bailable by the law*, or *not bailable*;—if "bailable by the law, then he was to be bailed "without any such letter;—if not bailable "by the law, then plainly the judges could "not have bailed him upon the letter, with-"out breach of their oath, which is, *that they* "*are to do justice according to the law, &c.*"—*State Trials*. 7. 175.

"So that, in bailing upon such offences "of the highest nature, a kind of discretion, "rather than a constant law, hath been ex-"ercised, when it stands *wholly indifferent* in "the eye of the court, whether the prisoner "be guilty or not." *Selden. St. Tr.* 7. 230. 1.

"I DENY that a man is always bailable, "when imprisonment is imposed upon him "for

"for cuſtody." *Attorney General Heath.* d°. 238.—By theſe quotations from the State Trials, though otherwiſe not of authority, it appears plainly that, in regard to *bailable* or *not bailable*, all parties agreed in admitting one propoſition as incontrovertible.

"IN relation to capital offences there are "eſpecially theſe acts of parliament that are "the common *landmarks* * touching offences "bailable or not bailable." *Hale.* 2. *P. C.* 127. The enumeration includes the ſeveral acts cited in this paper.

"PERSONS, taken with the *Manouvre*, are "not bailable, becauſe it is *furtum mani-* "*feſtum.*" *Hale.* 2. *P. C.* 133.

"THE writ of *Habeas Corpus* is of a high "nature; for if perſons be wrongfully com- "mitted, they are to be diſcharged upon this "writ returned; or, if bailable, they are to "be bailed;—*if not bailable, they are to be com-* "*mitted.*" *Hale.* 2. *P. C.* 143. This doct- rine of Lord Chief Juſtice Hale refers imme-

* It has been the ſtudy of Lord Manſfield to remove land-marks.

 diately

diately to the ſuperior courts from whence the writ iſſues.—"After the return is filed, the "court is either to diſcharge, or bail, or *com-* "*mit* him, as the nature of the cauſe re- "quires." *Hale.* 2. *P. C.* 146.

"If bail be granted, *otherwiſe than the law* "*alloweth*, the party that alloweth the ſame, "ſhall be fined, impriſoned, render damages, "or forfeit his place, as the caſe ſhall re- "quire." *Selden by N. Bacon.* 182.

"This induces an abſolute neceſſity of "expreſſing, upon every commitment, the "reaſon, for which it is made; that the "court, upon a *Habeas Corpus*, may examine "into its validity, and, *according to the cir-* "*cumſtances of the caſe*, may diſcharge, admit "to bail, or *remand* the priſoner." *Black-ſtone.* 3. 133.

"Marriot was committed for forging "indorſements upon bank bills, and, upon "a *Habeas Corpus*, was bailed, becauſe the "crime was only a great miſdemeanor;— "for though the forging the bills be felony, "yet forging the indorſement is not." *Sal-keld.* 1. 104.

"Appell-

"Appell de Mahem, &c. ideo ne fuit "lesse a baille, nient plus que in appell de "robbery ou murder; quod nota, et que in "robry et murder le partie n'est baillable." *Bro. Mainprise*. 67.

"The intendment of the law in bails is, "*quod stat indifferenter* whether he be guilty "or no; but, when he is convict by verdict "or confession, then he must be deemed in "law to be guilty of the felony, and therefore "*not bailable at all.*" *Coke*. 2. *Inst*. 188.— 4. 178.

"Bail is *quando stat indifferenter*, and *not* "when the offence is open and manifest." 2. *Inst*. 189.

"In this case *non stat indifferenter* whether "he be guilty or no, being taken with the "*Maner*, that is, with the thing stolen, as it "were in his hand." *D*o. *D*o.

"If it appeareth that this imprisonment "be just and lawful, he *shall* be *remanded* to "the former goaler; but, if it shall appear "to the court that he was imprisoned against

" the law of the land, they ought, by force
" of this ſtatute, to deliver him; if it be
" *doubtful*, and under conſideration, he may
" be bailed." 2. *Inſt.* 55.

It is unneceſſary to load the reader with any farther quotations. If theſe authorities are not deemed ſufficient to eſtabliſh the doctrine maintained in this paper, it will be in vain to appeal to the evidence of law-books, or to the opinions of judges. They are not the authorities, by which Lord Mansfield will abide. He aſſumes an arbitrary power of doing right; and, if he does wrong, it lies only between God and his conſcience.

Now, my Lord, although I have great faith in the preceding argument, I will not ſay, that every minute part of it is abſolutely invulnerable. I am too well acquainted with the practice of a certain court, directed by your example, as it is governed by your authority, to think there ever yet was an argument, however conformable to law and reaſon, in which a cunning, quibbling attorney might not diſcover a flaw. But, taking the whole of it together, I affirm that it conſtitutes a maſs of demonſtration, than which nothing more

compleat

compleat or ſatisfactory can be offered to the human mind. How an evaſive, indirect reply will ſtand with your reputation, or how far it will anſwer in point of defence at the bar of the houſe of lords, is worth your conſideration. If, after all that has been ſaid, it ſhould ſtill be maintained, that the court of King's Bench, in bailing felons, are exempted from all legal rules whatſoever, and that the judge has no direction to purſue, but his private affections, or mere unqueſtionable will and pleaſure, it will follow plainly, that the diſtinction between *bailable* and *not bailable*, uniformly expreſſed by the legiſlature, current through all our law-books, and admitted by all our great lawyers without exception, is in one ſenſe a nugatory, in another a pernicious diſtinction. It is nugatory, as it ſuppoſes a difference in the bailable quality of offences, when, in effect, the diſtinction refers only to the rank of the magiſtrate. It is pernicious, as it implies a rule of law, which yet the judge is not bound to pay the leaſt regard to, and impreſſes an idea upon the minds of the people, that the judge is wiſer and greater than the law.

It remains only to apply the law, thus ſtated, to the fact in queſtion. By an authentic copy of the *mittimus* it appears that John Eyre was committed for felony, plainly and ſpecially expreſſed in the warrant of commitment. He was charged before Alderman Halifax by the oath of Thomas Fielding, William Holder, William Payne, and William Naſh, for *feloniouſly ſtealing* eleven quires of writing-paper, value ſix ſhillings, the property of Thomas Beach, &c.—by the examinations, upon oath, of the four perſons mentioned in the *mittimus*, it was proved, that large quantities of paper had been miſſed, and that eleven quires (previouſly marked from a ſuſpicion that Eyre was the thief) were found upon him. Many other quires of paper, marked in the ſame manner, were found at his lodgings; and after he had been ſometime in Wood-ſtreet Compter, a key was found in his room there, which appeared to be a key to the cloſet at Guildhall, from whence the paper was ſtolen. When aſked what he had to ſay in his defence, his only anſwer was, *I hope you will bail me.* Mr. Holder, the Clerk, replied, *That is impoſſible. There never was an inſtance of it, when the*

the stolen goods were found upon the thief. The Lord Mayor was then applied to, and refused to bail him.—Of all these circumstances it was your duty to have informed yourself minutely. The fact was remarkable, and the chief magistrate of the city of London was known to have refused to bail the offender. To justify your compliance with the solicitations of your three countrymen, it should be proved that such allegations were offered to you, in behalf of their associate, as honestly and *bona fide* reduced it to a matter of doubt and indifference whether the prisoner was innocent or guilty.—Was any thing offered by the Scotch triumvirate that tended to invalidate the positive charge made against him by four credible witnesses upon oath? —Was it even insinuated to you, either by himself or his bail, that no felony was committed;—or that *he* was not the felon;—that the stolen goods were *not* found upon him;—or that he was only the receiver, not knowing them to be stolen?—Or, in short, did they attempt to produce any evidence of his insanity?—To all these questions, I answer for you, without the least fear of contradiction, positively NO. From the moment he was arrested, he never entertained any hope of acquittal; therefore thought of nothing but obtaining bail, that he might have time to ſettle his affairs, convey his fortune into another country, and ſpend the remainder of his life in comfort and affluence abroad. In this prudential ſcheme of future happineſs, the Lord Chief Juſtice of England moſt readily and heartily concurred. At ſight of ſo much virtue in diſtreſs, your natural benevolence took the alarm. Such a man as Mr. Eyre, ſtruggling with adverſity, muſt always be an intereſting ſcene to Lord Manſfield.—Or was it that liberal anxiety, by which your whole life has been diſtinguiſhed, to enlarge the liberty of the ſubject?—My Lord, we did not want this new inſtance of the liberality of your principles. We already knew what kind of ſubjects they were, for whoſe liberty you were anxious. At all events, the public are much indebted to you for fixing a price, at which felony may be committed with impunity. You bound a felon, notoriouſly worth thirty thouſand pounds, in the ſum of three hundred. With your natural turn to equity, and knowing, as you are, in the doctrine of precedents, you undoubtedly meant to ſettle the proportion

be-

between the fortune of the felon, and the fine, by which he may compound for his felony. The ratio now upon record, and transmitted to posterity under the auspices of Lord Mansfield, is exactly one to a hundred. —My Lord, without intending it, you have laid a cruel restraint upon the genius of your countrymen. In the warmest indulgence of their passions, they have an eye to the expence, and if their other virtues fail us, we have a resource in their œconomy.

By taking so trifling a security from John Eyre, you invited and manifestly exhorted him to escape. Although in bailable cases, it be usual to take four securities, you left him in the custody of three Scotchmen, whom he might have easily satisfied for conniving at his retreat. That he did not make use of the opportunity you industriously gave him neither justifies your conduct, nor can it be any way accounted for, but by his excessive and monstrous avarice. Any other man, but this bosom-friend of three Scotchmen, would gladly have sacrificed a few hundred pounds, rather than to submit to the infamy of pleading guilty in open court. It is possible indeed that he might have flattered himself, and

and not unreasonably, with the hopes of a pardon. That he would have been pardoned seems more than probable, if I had not directed the public attention to the leading step you took in favour of him. In the present gentle reign, we well know what use has been made of the lenity of the court and of the mercy of the crown. The Lord Chief Justice of England accepts of the hundredth part of the property of a felon taken in the fact, as a recognizance for his appearance. Your brother *Smythe* brow-beats a jury, and forces them to alter their verdict, by which they had found a Scotch serjeant guilty of murder; and though the Kennedies were convicted of a most deliberate and atrocious murder, they still had a claim to the royal mercy.—They were saved by the chastity of their connexions.—They had a sister; —yet it was not her beauty, but the pliancy of her virtue that recommended her to the King.—The holy author of our religion was seen in the company of sinners; but it was his gracious purpose to convert them from their sins. Another man, who in the ceremonies of our faith might give lessons to the great enemy of it, upon different principles keeps much the same company. He advertises

tises for patients, collects all the diseases of the heart, and turns a royal palace into an hospital for incurables.—A man of honour has no ticket of admission at St. James's. They receive him, like a virgin at the Magdalen's; —*Go thou and do likewise.*

MY charge against you is now made good. I shall however be ready to answer or to submit to fair objections. If, whenever this matter shall be agitated, you suffer the doors of the house of lords to be shut, I now protest, that I shall consider you as having made no reply. From that moment, in the opinion of the world, you will stand self-convicted. Whether your reply be quibbling and evasive, or liberal and in point, will be matter for the judgment of your peers;—but if, when every possible idea of disrespect to that noble house, (in whose honour and justice the nation implicitly confides) is here most solemnly disclaimed, you should endeavour to represent this charge, as a contempt of their authority, and move their lordships to censure the publisher of this paper, I then affirm that you support injustice by violence, that you are guilty of a heinous aggravation of your offence, and that you contribute

your

your utmoſt influence to promote, on the part of the higheſt court of judicature, a poſitive denial of juſtice to the nation.

JUNIUS.

LETTER LXIX.

TO THE RIGHT HON. LORD CAMDEN.

MY LORD,

I TURN with pleaſure, from that barren waſte, in which no ſalutary plant takes root, no verdure quickens, to a character fertile, as I willingly believe, in every great and good qualification. I call upon you, in the name of the Engliſh nation, to ſtand forth in defence of the laws of your country, and to exert, in the cauſe of truth and juſtice, thoſe great abilities, with which you were entruſted for the benefit of mankind. To aſcertain the facts, ſet forth in the preceding paper, it may be neceſſary to call the perſons, mentioned in the *mittimus*, to the bar of the houſe of lords. If a motion for that purpoſe ſhould be rejected, we ſhall know what

what to think of Lord Mansfield's innocence. The legal argument is submitted to your lordship's judgment. After the noble stand you made against Lord Mansfield upon the question of libel, we did expect that you would not have suffered that matter to have remained undetermined. But it was said that Lord Chief Justice Wilmot had been *prevailed upon* to vouch for an opinion of the late Judge Yates, which was supposed to make against you; and we admit of the excuse. When such detestable arts are employed to prejudge a question of right, it might have been imprudent, at that time, to have brought it to a decision. In the present instance you will have no such opposition to contend with. If there be a judge, or a lawyer of any note in Westminster-hall, who shall be daring enough to affirm that, according to the true intendment of the laws of England, a felon, taken with the *Maner*, *in flagranti delicto*, is bailable; or that the discretion of an English judge is merely arbitrary, and not governed by rules of law,—I should be glad to be acquainted with him. Whoever he be, I will take care that he shall not give you much trouble. Your lordship's character assures me that you will assume that principal part, which belongs to

you,

you, in ſupporting the laws of England, againſt a wicked judge, who makes it the occupation of his life, to miſinterpret and pervert them. If you decline this honourable office, I fear it will be ſaid that, for ſome months paſt, you have kept too much company with the Duke of Grafton. When the conteſt turns upon the interpretation of the laws, you cannot, without a formal ſurrender of all your reputation, yield the poſt of honour even to Lord Chatham. Conſidering the ſituation and abilities of Lord Mansfield, I do not ſcruple to affirm, with the moſt ſolemn appeal to God for my ſincerity, that, in *my* judgment, he is the very worſt and moſt dangerous man in the kingdom. Thus far I have done my duty in endeavouring to bring him to puniſhment. But mine is an inferior, miniſterial office in the temple of juſtice. —I have bound the victim, and dragged him to the altar.

JUNIUS.

THE Reverend Mr. John Horne having with his usual veracity and honest industry, circulated a report that Junius, in a letter to the Supporters of the Bill of Rights, had warmly declared himself in favour of long parliaments and rotten boroughs, it is thought necessary to submit to the public the following extract from his letter to John Wilkes, Esq; dated the 7th of September 1771, and laid before the society on the 24th of the same month.

"WITH regard to the several articles, "taken separately, I own I am concerned to "see that the great condition, which ought "to be the *sine quâ non* of parliamentary qua- "lification,—which ought to be the basis (as "it assuredly will be the only support) of every "barrier raised in defence of the constitution, "I mean *a declaration upon oath to shorten the* "*duration of parliaments*, is reduced to the "fourth rank in the esteem of the society; "and, even in that place, far from being in- "sisted on with firmness and vehemence, "seems to have been particularly slighted in "the

" the expression.—*You shall endeavour to restore*
" *annual parliaments!*—Are these the terms,
" which men, who are in earnest, make use
" of, when the *salus reipublicæ* is at stake?—
" I expected other language from Mr. Wilkes.
" —Besides my objection in point of form,
" I disapprove highly of the meaning of the
" fourth article as it stands. Whenever the
" question shall be seriously agitated, I will
" endeavour (and if I live will assuredly at-
" tempt it) to convince the English nation,
" by arguments to *my* understanding unan-
" swerable, that they ought to insist upon a
" triennial, and banish the idea of an annual
" parliament. . . . . I am con-
" vinced that, if shortening the duration of
" parliaments (which in effect is keeping the
" representative under the rod of the consti-
" tuent) be not made the basis of our new
" parliamentary jurisprudence, other checks
" or improvements signify nothing. On the
" contrary, if this be made the foundation,
" other measures may come in aid, and, as
" auxiliaries, be of considerable advantage.
" Lord Chatham's project, for instance, of
" increasing the number of knights of shires,
" appears to me admirable. . . . . . As to
" cutting away the rotten boroughs, I am
" as

" as much offended as any man at ſeeing ſo
" many of them under the direct influence
" of the crown, or at the diſpoſal of private
" perſons. Yet, I own, I have both doubts
" and apprehenſions, in regard to the remedy
" you propoſe. I ſhall be charged perhaps
" with an unuſual want of political intrepidity,
" when I honeſtly confeſs to you, that I am
" ſtartled at the idea of ſo extenſive an ampu-
" tation.—In the firſt place, I queſtion the
" power, *de jure*, of the legiſlature to disfran-
" chiſe a number of boroughs, upon the ge-
" neral ground of improving the conſtitution.
" There cannot be a doctrine more fatal to
" the liberty and property we are contending
" for, than that, which confounds the idea of
" a *ſupreme* and an *arbitrary* legiſlature. I need
" not point out to you the fatal purpoſes, to
" which it has been, and may be applied. If
" we are ſincere in the political creed we pro-
" feſs, there are many things, which we ought
" to affirm, cannot be done by King, Lords
" and Commons. Among theſe I reckon the
" disfranchiſing of boroughs with a general
" view of improvement. I conſider it as equi-
" valent to robbing the parties concerned of
" their freehold, of their birth-right. I ſay
" that, although this birth-right may be for-
" feited, or the exerciſe of it ſuſpended in

" particular cafes, it cannot be taken away,
" by a general law, for any real or pretended
" purpofe of improving the conftitution. Sup-
" pofing the attempt made, I am perfuaded
" you cannot mean that either King, or Lords
" fhould take an active part in it. A bill,
" which only touches the reprefentation of
" the people, muft originate in the houfe of
" commons. In the formation and mode of
" paffing it, the exclufive right of the com-
" mons muft be afferted as fcrupuloufly, as in
" the cafe of a money-bill. Now, Sir, I
" fhould be glad to know by what kind of
" reafoning it can be proved, that there is a
" power vefted in the reprefentative to deftroy
" his immediate conftituent. From whence
" could he poffibly derive it? A courtier, I
" know, will be ready to maintain the affirm-
" ative. The doctrine fuits him exactly,
" becaufe it gives an unlimited operation to
" the influence of the crown. But we, Mr.
" Wilkes, ought to hold a different language.
" It is no anfwer to me to fay, that the bill,
" when it paffes the houfe of commons, is the
" act of the majority, and not the reprefenta-
" tives of the particular boroughs concerned.
" If the majority can disfranchife ten bo-
" roughs, why not twenty, why not the whole
" kingdom? Why fhould not they make their
" own

" own ſeats in parliament for life?—When
" the ſeptennial act paſſed, the legiſlature did
" what, apparently and palpably, they had no
" power to do; but they did more than people
" in general were aware of: they, in effect,
" disfranchiſed the whole kingdom for four
" years.

" For argument's ſake, I will now ſup-
" poſe, that the expediency of the meaſure,
" and the power of parliament are unqueſt-
" ionable. Still you will find an inſurmount-
" able difficulty in the execution. When all
" your inſtruments of amputation are pre-
" pared, when the unhappy patient lies bound
" at your feet, without the poſſibility of re-
" ſiſtance, by what infallible rule will you
" direct the operation?—When you propoſe
" to cut away the *rotten* parts, can you tell
" us what parts are perfectly *ſound?*—Are
" there any certain limits, in fact or theory,
" to inform you at what point you muſt
" ſtop, at what point the mortification ends.
" To a man ſo capable of obſervation and
" reflection as you are, it is unneceſſary to
" ſay all that might be ſaid upon the ſub-
" ject. Beſides that I approve highly of
" Lord Chatham's idea *of infuſing a portion*
" *of new health into the conſtitution to enable*

" *it to bear its infirmities*, (a brilliant expreſ-
" ſion, and full of intrinſic wiſdom) other
" reaſons concur in perſuading me to adopt
" it. I have no objection, &c.

THE man, who fairly and compleatly anſwers this argument, ſhall have my thanks and my applauſe. My heart is already with him.—I am ready to be converted.—I admire his morality, and would gladly ſubſcribe to the articles of his faith.—Grateful, as I am, to the GOOD BEING, whoſe bounty has imparted to me this reaſoning intellect, whatever it is, I hold myſelf proportionably indebted to him, from whoſe inlightened underſtanding another ray of knowledge communicates to mine. But neither ſhould I think the moſt exalted faculties of the human mind, a gift worthy of the divinity; nor any aſſiſtance, in the improvement of them, a ſubject of gratitude to my fellow creature, if I were not ſatisfied, that really to inform the underſtanding corrects and enlarges the heart.

JUNIUS.

FINIS.